PAUL
AND HIS MESSAGE
FOR LIFE'S JOURNEY

PAUL
AND HIS MESSAGE
FOR LIFE'S JOURNEY

by

William G. Thompson, S.J.

Paulist Press
New York ■ Mahwah

Library of Congress Cataloging-in-Publication Data

Thompson, William G.
    Paul's message for life's journey.

    1. Bible. N.T. Epistles of Paul—Criticism, inter-
pretation, etc. 2. Paul, the Apostle, Saint. I. Title.
BS2650.2.T55   1986   225.9'24   86-9506
ISBN 0-8091-2824-1 (pbk.)

Published by Paulist Press
997 Macarthur Boulevard
Mahwah, New Jersey 07430

Printed and bound in the
United States of America

Contents

*Dedicated to
All Adult Learners*

Acknowledgements

Timothy E. O'Connell is Director of the Institute of Pastoral Studies at Chicago's Loyola University. He graciously reduced my teaching responsibilities and enabled me to coordinate my teaching with writing this book.

New Testament colleagues will recognize how much I have depended on their scholarship, especially Paul J. Achtemeier, Joseph A. Fitzmyer, Leander Keck, Wayne Meeks, Robin Scroggs, David Stanley, and Krister Stendahl.

David C. Reeves explored with me how to find meaning in Paul through his symbols, metaphors, and story. James W. Fowler, along with Evelyn E. and James A. Whitehead, introduced me to how patterns in adult development can make Paul more accessible to contemporary readers.

From her experience in spiritual direction, Mary Sharon Riley, R.C. contributed the cases of people praying with Paul's letters and companioned me in planning and writing the book.

I especially thank Dolores Ready for her interest in the book from the beginning, for her valuable advice about its overall shape, and for her editing which brought the manuscript closer to its intended readers.

I dedicate this book to the adults whom I have been privileged to teach—young and old, men and women, seminarians and jubilarians, Protestant and Catholic, lay and religious, ordained and non-ordained. Fifteen years of mutual teaching and learning have moved me to write about Paul, the man and his letters. I am grateful.

Prologue:

Perspectives on Paul and a Preview of This Book

In workshops and courses with adults I often hear these questions: How can we get started with Paul? Why does he seem so unapproachable? Why is his message so difficult to understand? Can it have meaning for our lives? Why is praying with the Gospels so much easier than with Paul's letters? Are there methods that can help us pray with Paul? In this book I respond to these questions by inviting you to dialogue with Paul, to find meaning in his message, and to pray with his letters.

In my youth I knew neither Paul nor his letters. But as a young adult, I was introduced to Paul by a great man who had come to appreciate Paul's human qualities. In a sermon entitled, "Saint Paul's Gift of Sympathy," John Henry Newman described Paul as having extraordinary knowledge and love of what being human means: Paul loved his brothers and sisters in Christ, and he lived in them. He felt with them and for them, and he was often anxious for them. He helped them, but he also turned to them for comfort. He rejoiced with those who were rejoicing, and he wept with those who were weeping. Paul was weak with the weak, strong with the strong, and he gloried in his own infirmities. Newman's portrait of Paul has informed all my later work on the man and his letters.

Prior to my ordination to the priesthood we seminarians studied Paul's letters in relation to Catholic doctrine. We approached them with questions that originated more from post-Reformation debates than from Paul's concrete experience in his historical situation. We combed the letters for what might prove and support traditional Roman Catholic teaching about faith and revelation, sin and grace, the person and work of Christ, the Church and its sacraments, and the final judgment.

We ignored the distance in time and culture that separated Paul from later creeds and doctrine. We failed to recognize how different his symbols and metaphors are from later technical language and systematic

1

thought. As a result, Paul's message seemed more static than dynamic, more conceptual than imaginative. It appealed more to the mind than to the heart.

As we studied Paul through later doctrines, we concluded that his letters were too complicated for us to use in liturgy or religious education. Instead, we focused on the Gospels. Both Paul and his letters had become so sterile and distant that we did not appreciate them or feel confident in using them. They seemed divorced from our experience and totally inaccessible.

I began to investigate Paul in his historical context in my doctoral studies at the Biblical Institute in Rome. With the available data, we reconstructed Paul's situation and worked to understand his letters in their original context. We studied Paul's message against his Jewish-Hellenistic background and in the light of his experience with concrete Christian communities. We imagined Paul relating to each community, and we tried to listen to his letter as the original recipients might have heard it. In taking a more historical approach, we freed Paul and his letters from the confines of later creeds and doctrine.

For the past eighteen years, I have taught Paul and his letters in courses, workshops, and prayer-study weekends. Presenting the letters on their own terms, I have not been concerned about how they might prove or support creeds or doctrine. I have explored Paul's personal experience and his work as missionary to the Gentiles. I have blended my deep appreciation of Paul with my respect for the distance that separates us in time and culture.

However, as I taught, I began to sense that the adult students and I were not totally satisfied with understanding Paul and his letters in their original situation. We also wanted to know what they might mean for us as Christian adults in today's world. Repeatedly we asked ourselves if Paul could transcend the distance that separates us to inform and influence our lives. Could we interact with Paul and his letters? Could we expect them to help us find meaning in our contemporary experience?

Having wrestled with these important questions, I am convinced that Paul *can* inform and influence how we live as Christians. Through his symbols and metaphors, we can bridge the distance that separates us from Paul. For with these symbols and metaphors Paul constructs a world of meaning into which he invites us. If we accept his invitation, Paul will show us where we came from, describe where we are now, and tell us where we are going.

But one final question remained for me and my students: Could we pray with Paul's letters? I must confess that until recently I have found praying with the Gospels easier than praying with Paul's letters. I enjoy listening to a Gospel passage and attending to the Lord in the story. Entering into a Gospel scene with my mind and imagination to encounter the Lord seems so simple. For Jesus seems immediately available in the Gospels.

Praying with Paul, however, has seemed much more complicated, because Jesus neither speaks nor acts in Paul's letters. Paul does not tell stories about Jesus' miracles or His conflicts with the Jewish religious authorities. He does not recount Jesus' parables or His instructions to His followers. Instead, Paul makes statements, often difficult to understand, about God's action in Jesus Christ. Yet, despite this, I have been drawn in recent years to pray with Paul's letters, especially with passages that disclose the paradox of power in apparent weakness. Perhaps my prayer now reflects the mid-life journey I have made with Paul.

You see, I have learned that Paul can accompany us throughout our life's journey. As children we loved stories with concrete scenes and dramatic action. Children are more drawn to stories about Paul than to dialoguing with him or finding meaning in his message. They like the longer stories in the Acts of the Apostles about Paul persecuting Christians, about his dramatic conversion on the road to Damascus, about his exploits as a missionary to the Gentiles and community organizer, about his trials in Jerusalem and Caesarea Maritima, and about his hazardous sea voyage to Rome. But children are probably not able to relate to the symbols and metaphors with which Paul articulates his message.

Young adults respond to the expectations and judgments of significant others, such as spouses, respected persons at work, Church or political authorities. If they react positively to his temperament and personality, Paul can become a significant other for them. Through dialogue they can develop empathy for Paul and, through that empathy, be drawn to his message. Fascinated by Paul's struggles to defend his authority as an apostle and the truth of his Gospel, young adults can also find meaning in symbols like the body of Christ, in metaphors like reconciliation, and in the hymn to love (1 Cor 13).

But as adults take more responsibility for individualizing their lives, they resonate with Paul's situation after his experience of the risen Lord: his fellow Pharisees consider him a traitor; some Christians continue to see him as a former persecutor; and the Romans tolerate him as they tolerate all other Jews. Without much support Paul remains convinced that he is an apostle of Jesus Christ and that his Gospel is salvation for Jews and for Gentiles.

As mature adults move away from their conventional worlds in which they have responded to the expectations of others, they begin to resonate with Paul's move away from Pharisaic Judaism. They tend to interpret Paul's polarities in either/or terms, and they are drawn to the metaphors that express sharp dichotomies (for example, from alienation to reconciliation, from slavery to freedom, from danger to salvation). For these dichotomies reflect how they make meaning in their own adult lives.

In their middle years adults begin to experience a richer and deeper resonance with Paul's message. More alive to the paradoxes and polarities in life and more willing to live with complexity and ambiguity, they discover that dialoguing with Paul and finding meaning in his message is easier. Experience has taught them the meaning of defeat and disappointment. They have tasted the demands of irreversible commitments. They have faced paradoxes such as life in death, hope in despair, joy in suffering, power in weakness.

Moving through our adult years means spending long periods of time in transition. Concrete events combine with an inner readiness to precipitate such transitions. Our hopes and dreams are fulfilled, or we watch them fail. Significant people remain faithful in their love and care, or they betray our relationship. Conflicts arise in our personal and professional lives that introduce more doubt and confusion than clarity and certitude. In such times we confront our weakness and vulnerability, and we must choose between denying the pain in our experience or remaining open to where it might lead us. Paul's message with its emphasis on trusting the power of God and on dying and rising in Christ can support us as we struggle to find meaning in these normal adult transitions.

Preview of this Book

Having studied and dialogued and prayed and grown with Paul, I want to share with you my appreciation of the man and his message. I hope that Paul will become more accessible to you by enabling you to dialogue with him, to find meaning in his message and to pray with his letters.

The three major sections of this book develop these three perspectives on Paul. In Part I we dialogue with Paul's experience as a diaspora Jew and a Pharisee of the Pharisees (Chapter 1), in his experience of the risen Lord (Chapter 2), as a missionary to the Gentiles and a community organizer (Chapter 3), and as a letter writer (Chapter 4). As we articulate resemblances and differences between Paul's experience and our own, we reflect on their implications for our personal and professional lives.

In Part II, entitled "Finding Meaning in Paul's Message," we study Paul's message and explore how it might explain our religious past, address our present, and orient us toward the future. We ask how Paul's message might enable us to find coherence and meaning in our lives. First we consider the theme "Dying and Rising in Christ" (Chapter 5). We look at God's action in Jesus Christ crucified and risen, and at how Christians participate in that action. Topics include power in weakness, death and resurrection, equality-community-Eucharist, dynamics of suffering, vision of the future. Reflecting on this aspect of Paul's message may enable us to find meaning in apparently meaningless suffering.

In dealing with Paul's understanding of "God's Plan of Action for the World" (Chapter 6), we focus on how it enabled him to find meaning in the apparent conflict between God's promises to Israel and his mission to the Gentiles. Topics include Adam and Christ, the Jewish law, Abraham—faith in the promise, and salvation for Gentiles and Jews. We reflect on what Paul can teach us about finding meaning in similar conflicts.

In studying "Individuals and Communities in the New Age" (Chapter 7), we focus on how Paul understands the effects of God's action in Christ in persons of faith. We note especially the metaphors Paul uses to express these effects. We ask what power these metaphors might or might not have to help us find meaning in our own lives. We then study the process that Paul describes for discovering the action of the Spirit. We again reflect on what we might learn for our everyday lives.

In Part III, "Praying with Paul's Letters," we listen to what Paul says about prayer and learn from his practice. We grow more familiar with the prayers in Paul's letters. And we reflect on how prayer can be a place to dialogue with Paul and find meaning in his message (Chapter 8). We also present cases of persons praying with Paul and describe methods appropriate to his letters (Chapter 9).

In the Appendix, entitled "Paul and Women," we study Paul's attitude toward women as distinct from that of the later Pauline tradition. We focus on the texts that disclose Paul's view and reflect on the developments that took place after his martyrdom. We also ask what implications Paul's view might have for contemporary women's issues.

Before moving on, I invite you to reflect on your experience of Paul and his message. I suggest that you spend some time with the following questions:

■ Right *now* what prompts you to read this book about Paul? What persons, recent events, experiences?
■ In the past where have you encountered Paul and his message? In prayer, in a course, in a retreat, in an adult education program, at church?
■ Write down all the experiences you have had with Paul, and then for

each experience try to remember how it felt. Was it a good or bad experience? Did you like or dislike it? Why?

■ Finally, complete the following sentence with adjectives, pictures, or other creative responses: "At this moment my relationship to Paul is best described as _____."

Part I

DIALOGUING WITH PAUL

I am convinced that meaningful dialogue is possible with Paul, that we can interact with him through his letters, and that his experience can influence how we live as Christians. But not everyone shares these convictions. Some would argue that Paul remains an interesting historical personage. While he may have been a great missionary, he is distant from us in his personality and temperament, in his background and culture, in his conversion experience, and in his call to the Gentiles. Dialogue cannot happen across such a distance.

If this is so, why have Christians in every age found in Paul an inspiration for their lives? And can he inspire and influence us today? I believe that the answer to this all-important question is yes. But first of all, we must respect all that separates us from Paul. We must let him stand apart in his personality and temperament, in his historical situation, in his background and culture, in his conversion experience, and in his call. And we must stand apart form Paul in our own unique historical circumstances. Only then can we dialogue with Paul, as we dialogue with any other person, by listening and responding.

In his letters Paul tells us about his experience, and we respond by sharing our experience. Paul interacted with his concrete historical situation, and we interact with our concrete historical situation. We can respond to him, because in any situation we confront the same basic human tensions, such as death and life, despair and hope, humiliation and exaltation, destruction and creation, power and weakness, unity and diversity, masculine and feminine. Paul met these polarities in situations very different from ours. But in listening to Paul tell us how he and his communities learned to live with these basic human tensions we begin to imagine new possibilities for dealing with the same polarities today. Dialoguing with Paul informs our lives because it touches the deepest bond between us, namely, our shared humanity.

In interacting with Paul we try not to project onto him what we would like him to say or do. Instead, we let him speak so that we might listen. As we listen, we watch for resemblances between Paul and ourselves, since the resemblances disclose how Paul can become a paradigm for our lives. As a paradigm, Paul informs and influences our lives as individuals and communities. Informing our lives means more than giving us data or information. And certainly it does not mean his telling us what to believe or how to act. Rather, it suggests a basic formation of vision and values. Influencing us means letting Paul enter into the mainstream of our lives to help us live as Christians in our unique historical situation. As we dialogue with Paul, we must never lose sight of the fact that our time and culture are different from his and that our capacities and powers are distinctive.

Now to begin—

■ What surfaces in you when you hear the name, Paul of Tarsus?
■ What adjectives describe him?
■ What nouns do you associate with him?
■ What do you think about him?
■ How do you feel?

Adjectives for Paul that I most often hear include *committed, strong, energetic, stubborn, challenging, exciting, profound, passionate, complicated, obsessive, faith-filled, zealous, weak, compassionate, independent, clever, fearless, hopeful, angry, affectionate.* Nouns frequently associated with Paul include *journey, law, scholar, fighter, chauvinist, revolutionary, paradox, love-hate, conversion, suffering, globe-trotter, tentmaker, workaholic, fool for Christ.* Some people are attracted to Paul; others are repelled. Some are captivated by his commitment to Christ and his missionary zeal. Others are disgusted by his attitude toward women. Few remain neutral.

In dialoguing with Paul, we confront and interact with the man in his historical situation. We study and reflect on his life as a diaspora Jew and Pharisee of the Pharisees (Chapter One), on his experience of the risen Lord (Chapter Two), on his work as missionary to the Gentiles and community organizer (Chapter Three), and on his letter-writing (Chapter Four). Each facet of Paul's experience discloses the man in his historical situation. Each invites us to listen and learn. No one facet paints a full picture, nor do all of them together succeed in capturing the complex multi-dimensional man that was Paul of Tarsus. As we reconstruct each aspect of Paul, we listen for how he might inform and influence our lives.

1

Diaspora Jew and
Pharisee of the Pharisees

I magine a diaspora—a marginal, ethnic, refugee
or minority community in your city. How would
you describe their life together? What is their attitude toward their
homeland? How do they relate to the dominant, majority culture around
them? How do the different generations relate to each other as they adapt
to life away from home?

Twenty years ago Consuelo and Julian Parra came to Chicago from
Cuba with their eldest daughter, Teresita. Three other children were
born in this country: a son, Julian, and twin daughters, Lourdes and
Maria. Consuelo's parents came with them, as did her sister, Zeyda.
Today the grandparents speak only Spanish. Consuelo and Julian speak
English with a heavy Cuban accent. Teresita has reluctantly learned
Spanish, since she considers herself an American. The three younger
children speak both Spanish and English with no trace of an accent.
Consuelo and Julian work very hard to provide educational opportunities
for their children, and their children are responsible to them for making
the most of their education. After graduation from college, Teresita
married a man of Polish descent. They are expecting their first child.
The Parras live in the "diaspora," that is, away from their homeland in
Cuba and and in the dominant, foreign culture of Chicago.

Paul was born away from Palestine in Tarsus, the capital of the
Roman province of Cilicia in Asia Minor. He was raised in a Jewish
diaspora community, not unlike the one portrayed in "Fiddler on the
Roof." Archeologists have found Jewish synagogues, cemeteries, and
other buildings strewn across the Roman Empire. These remains witness
to Jews who established communities like the community at Tarsus
throughout the empire. Scholars estimate that in the second half of the
first century the Jewish population away from Palestine far exceeded
that of the homeland. Social and economic opportunities, largely trade
related, had drawn these Jews away from Palestine.

9

Diaspora Jews made legal arrangements with their Greek leaders and later with their Roman rulers to protect their distinctive way of life. With these safeguards Jews found that living as minority communities in the foreign Greco-Roman culture was an advantage. Since their legal status allowed them to gather in homes and synagogues for religious purposes, quasi-autonomous Jewish communities could be found in almost every major Hellenistic city.

Paul's family belonged to such a community in Tarsus, a center of Hellenistic culture, philosophy, and education. Its schools surpassed those of Athens and Alexandria. Its population enjoyed a high level of culture. Paul received his early education in this environment with all the opportunities that the Hellenistic city provided. He learned Greek, exposed himself to the philosophy taught in the schools, and absorbed the religious mood and world view. But above all, Paul grew deeply convinced that he was a Jew, that he was a Hebrew born of Hebrews who belonged to the people of Israel and to the tribe of Benjamin. He cherished his Jewish heritage precisely because the dominant Hellenistic culture tended to challenge rather than support his traditions. Being Jewish was far from fashionable in Tarsus. It brought few rewards. Within this tension Paul gained a strong sense of his Jewish identity but also remained open to the Hellenistic world. He began to lay the foundation for his later work as a Christian missionary to the Gentiles.

Jews in the diaspora maintained lively contact with their homeland. By the emperor's decree they were free to make pilgrimages to the temple in Jerusalem. Much to the chagrin of local magistrates, they collected large amounts of money and abundant offerings for pilgrims to take to the holy city. Diaspora Jews also built their synagogues facing the temple in Jerusalem. Their concern to orient themselves toward their native land distinguished Jews from other religious groups in the Hellenistic world.

Despite the contact with Palestine, diaspora Jews developed different religious attitudes and practices from those of the Jews at home. They showed less concern for the destiny and fortunes of their native land, since for them the traditional ties between religion and homeland had been cut. Jerusalem and its temple remained a central site of pilgrimage and an object of sentimental attachment. But diaspora Jews found themselves reevaluating their traditional beliefs about God's unique presence in the temple. They also focused on religion more as a matter of individual salvation than as a concern for national prosperity. The chief religious figure was their local synagogue leader, not the high priest in the temple. As prophet and guide, this local leader interpreted for his diaspora community what living as faithful Jews outside Palestine meant.

At his synagogue lessons in Tarsus, Paul learned to see Judaism more as a religion of individual salvation than as a religion of national prosperity. He came to value creeds and law codes, since they were much more present than the distant rituals and sacrifices of the temple. For Paul, as for all diaspora Jews, Judaism transcended its homeland to find a home in cities like Tarsus. What he learned as a boy in Tarsus informed his later conviction that Jew and Gentile were one in Christ.

In Paul's day the religious mood in the Mediterranean world can be best described as "a failure of nerve" and a "climate of anxiety." Despite, or perhaps because of, the fact that isolated city-states had begun to interact with each other through wider trade routes and new opportunities for travel and the old structures of the city-state had been shattered, people felt more rootless than rooted, more insecure than secure. As men and women began to see themselves as citizens of a huge Greco-Roman Empire, they also began to feel lost, helpless, and naked. They suffered from a cosmic paranoia. Dangers seemed everywhere. The heavens seemed hostile, and the world more like a prison than a home. People longed to escape to another world, and they yearned for a hero-savior to show them the way out. Exiled from their true home, the Beyond, they wanted to know how they might return to that world-beyond-this-world, to the god-beyond-the-god-of-this-world. Hellenistic religions responded to their deep longing for escape by making salvation their major concern.

In Tarsus, Paul encountered this cultural pessimism about life in this world. He saw how the dominant mood called for deep, personal conviction and for strong loyalty to a savior and guide who would teach his followers how to escape. Paul the Jew agreed that human history was rushing toward a foreordained tragic end. But since God still ruled creation, Paul was also convinced that present struggles were necessary to introduce a new age of salvation. God would intervene to transform the world. The Jews as God's people would be forever blessed because of their fidelity, and their enemies would be forever punished. In the meantime, the chosen people must endure the struggles, prepare for the new age, and watch for the signs of its coming. Paul later preached that the new age began with the death and resurrection of Jesus Christ, that it will be completed at his second coming, and that in the meantime those who believe are already saved from this world but not yet fully saved.

Without forgetting the distance in time or the differences in culture that separate us from Paul, we may find resemblances between his diaspora origins and our contemporary situation. In Tarsus Paul grew more convinced of his Jewish heritage through dialogue with the dominant

Hellenistic culture. We too might be called to act out our Christian faith and values in a society to which we cannot conform. We may come to know ourselves as diaspora people in our own land.

For example, we who believe in Jesus Christ may at times experience tension and conflict, even challenge and ridicule from the culture around us. In the work place, we may feel like foreigners in a strange land. We try to serve others more than seek money or power for ourselves. Rather than isolate ourselves from others through self-centered competition, we work to create a climate of cooperation. We dare to be different, and we are often criticized. But in being true to our values, we also grow in our Christian faith.

In Tarsus Paul encountered the widespread pessimism about life in the world. Some people say that today we have begun to experience a new confidence, a new optimism in our country with an upswing in the economy and increasing prosperity. Others are more pessimistic in pointing out the escalating arms race, international terrorism, the drug culture, disruption in marriage and family life, an increase in violence and crime. Still others see us tottering between optimism and pessimism. We do well to ask how our contemporary mood might resemble the pessimism that Paul encountered in the Hellenistic world and whether a religion focused on salvation might respond to that mood.

Pharisee of the Pharisees

Paul first came to know Judaism in his home and in the synagogue in Tarsus. Then, as a young man, he moved to Jerusalem and lived as a Pharisee. He trained to become a teacher of the law under Gamaliel, and he became a recognized teacher in his own right, for the Jewish Sanhedrin would later give him authority to persecute the Christians in Damascus.

By moving from Tarsus to Jerusalem, from diaspora to homeland, Paul enlarged his view of Judaism. Jews in Palestine tied their religion to the land and centered it in the feasts and sacrifices at the temple. For the first time Paul participated in those great celebrations—Passover and Tabernacles, Atonement and Dedication. His previous dedication to the law became balanced with a new appreciation of ritual worship in the temple.

Paul also understood himself as a thoroughgoing Pharisee. In Tarsus he came to cherish creeds and law codes. In Jerusalem he pursued his dedication to perfection according to the law: "... as to the law a Pharisee ... as to righteousness under the law blameless" (Phil 3:5-6).

In its origins, the Pharisaic movement was made up of laymen, particularly lay scribes. It was intended to and did in fact respond to religious needs within Judaism. The movement succeeded especially well among townspeople, that is, among the middle-class artisans, traders, officials, and other service people who emerged from the impact of Hellenistic culture. The original Pharisees understood Judaism to go beyond the temple. They challenged the power of the landed aristocracy and rejected compromise with Rome. They developed a detailed program whereby a Jewish man and his family could maintain their identity no matter where they lived and in any walk of life. The Pharisees drew up detailed legislation on how to fulfill regulations such as sabbath observances, dietary laws, and tithing. They drew on the written Pentateuch but also on a second oral law that they believed God gave Moses on Mount Sinai. Through extensive oral commentary the Pharisees brought the law closer to the Jewish people in their everyday lives.

Critics often accuse the Pharisees of transforming Judaism into a legislative system with exclusive emphasis on external observance of the law. But a genuine religious concern guided them to see the law not as a burden but as an instruction for daily life. For the Pharisees showed how the law was given to faithful Jews as the foundation for their way through life no matter what their situation or occupation. The Pharisees were respected and influential precisely because of their concern for the people.

The Pharisees insisted on fulfilling the letter of the law. But they knew that no set of statutes, no matter how detailed, could cover every concrete situation. In their response to new experiences or dilemmas not covered by traditional laws, the Pharisees can seem hair-splitting, even ridiculous in their interpretations. But they intended to create a total way of life that was blessed with the blessings promised in the law.

Not all the Jews in Palestine and the diaspora were prepared to live according to the Pharisaic system. Pharisees themselves often found their system difficult to adhere to and so came together in associations to support each other in striving for perfection according to the law. These associations maintained strict rules of admission and expected their members to observe the law as perfectly as possible.

Pharisees clashed with other Jews who could not accept their views, but they continued to play an important role in Judaism. For example, they legislated for the temple rituals, even though the Sadducees had charge of the sacrifices and festivals. When the Romans destroyed the temple (AD 70), Pharisees assumed almost exclusive power in Judea. Without the temple, synagogues remained the center of Jewish life, since they could more easily be rebuilt. The Jewish priests no longer offered sacrifices in Jerusalem, but the law remained intact. Pharisees retained their popularity with the people by playing a significant role in the postwar reconstruction.

As a Pharisee, Paul intensified the dedication to the law that he had learned in Tarsus. Because the law centered his life, he strove to observe it perfectly. By his own achievements, his works, Paul earned and maintained that relationship with God. In his zeal for perfect observance Paul was in charge of his relationship to God. He controlled his successes and failures. In a word, Paul was a true Pharisee of the Pharisees.

Paul devoted his energies to fulfilling the law as interpreted by the Pharisees. He may also have found support in his striving by associating with other Pharisees. Perhaps Paul came to see the law as a set of regulations divorced from the covenant love and fidelity between God and the chosen people. But one thing is certain: the law was the center through which Paul communicated with God.

Paul the Pharisee demonstrated his zeal for the law by persecuting those who belonged to the young Christian movement. He persecuted them in Jerusalem. He entered their homes, dragged off men and women, and committed them to prison. He was entrusted to do the same in Damascus. With strong threats he set out on the journey, but on the way he encountered the risen Lord. That encounter marked the end of the law as the center of Paul's life.

Does Paul's life as a Pharisee resemble our experience? It makes me recall how I learned the difference between right and wrong. We emphasized laws, works and achievements, earning and striving for salvation, hoping for rewards and fearing punishment. We learned rules and regulations that resemble what the Pharisees taught. We knew what was right, and we knew what was wrong. Salvation depended on how well we observed those laws. We wrestled with them, played games with them, and found ways to get around them. We focused more on the rules and regulations than on a loving God.

Sin meant that we violated a law, as we violated civil laws. We accused ourselves before the priest-judge. He imposed a penance and absolved us from our sins. We resolved to observe the rules and regulations with greater care, since they were the sure guide to eternal salvation.

For me, as a youth, God seemed a lawgiver who threatened to punish us for failing to obey the divine laws and promised to reward us for our successes. Progress depended on our works and achievements, our striving to live by God's rules and regulations. Growing into a deep personal relationship with such an overpowering God was a very difficult, perhaps well-nigh impossible.

Again, I invite you to spend some time reflecting on Paul's experience and your own:

■ Do you think the contemporary mood of our country is pessimistic? Why or why not?
■ Where can we have optimism?
■ Do rules and regulations stand at the center of your relationship with God?
■ Do you resonate with Paul's striving for perfection according to the law?
■ What other resemblances surface between you and Paul the Pharisee?
■ Has something happened to you that moved rules and regulations to the periphery of your life?
■ What image do you have of rules and regulations and yourself?

2

Experience of the Risen Lord

What surfaces when you hear the word conversion? In popular use it often suggests that persons have turned their backs on a life of sin to begin living more virtuous lives. Or it means that they have changed from one religion to another or from one denomination to another. Conversion is also used to name Paul's experience of the risen Lord, the experience that changed him from a Pharisee dedicated to the law to a missionary of Jesus Christ to the Gentiles. But in this conversion, Paul did not turn his back on a life of sin, nor did he cease thinking of himself as a Jew. So we must determine in what sense his experience of the risen Lord can be called a conversion.

Before the experience Paul was convinced that he was a Jew, and he was proud of his Jewish heritage. That conviction and pride remained until he died. He never considered himself anything but a Jew who related to the same God of Israel. The law might cease to be at the center of his life. He might give up his identity as a Pharisee. But he never rejected the fact that he was of the people of Israel, of the tribe of Benjamin, a Hebrew born of Hebrews.

When God revealed Jesus Christ as Son, God turned Paul's life in a new direction. Paul continued to worship and serve the same God of Israel. But he accepted a new center through whom to communicate with God. As a Pharisee, he had cherished the law and striven to be blameless in his observance. Now he let go of the law to embrace Jesus Christ as Lord. For God revealed that Jesus Christ was to be at the center of their relationship and that Paul was to preach him to the Gentiles. Jesus Christ became the means through whom God related to Paul and in whom Paul was to live out his relationship to the God of Israel.

With that new center Paul also let go of former values. He had seen works of the law as personal achievements by which he earned and kept his relationship with God. Now he realized that his relationship with

God was a pure gift. As a Pharisee, he controlled how he stood with God by his individual successes or failures in observing the law. But now, made aware of his own weakness, he accepted Jesus Christ as the power who lived within him. Unable to save himself, Paul let go and let God make Jesus Christ the center of his life and faith his central value.

Paul also received a new mission. As a Pharisee, he had promoted the law as the way to God. Now he relinquished his former position with its prestige and privilege to serve the communities of Christians that he had persecuted. He understood that God wanted him to preach Jesus Christ to Gentiles who were to be saved without adopting the law. No longer was the law important. For Jews and Gentiles had equal access to God in Jesus Christ. Judaism was no longer rooted in the law but in the person of Jesus Christ.

We can summarize Paul's "transition" in the following scheme:

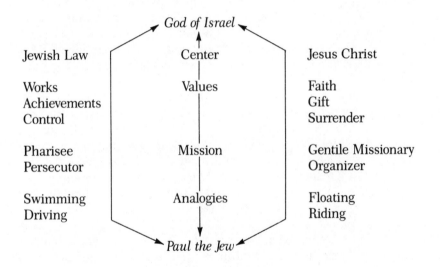

Paul describes how he experienced the risen Lord in his letter to the Galatians.

> For you have heard of my former life in Judaism, how I persecuted the Church of God violently and tried to destroy it; and I advanced in Judaism beyond many of my own age among my people, so extremely zealous was I for the traditions of my fathers. But when he who had set me apart before I was born, and had called me through his grace, was pleased to reveal his Son to me,

> in order that I might preach him among the Gentiles,
> I did not confer with flesh and blood, nor did I go up to
> Jerusalem to those who were apostles before me, but I
> went away into Arabia; and again I returned to Damascus
> (Gal 1:13-17).

Paul is convinced that God planned this revelation from his birth. His language associates his experience with that of Jeremiah (1:5) and Isaiah (49:1). God took the initiative. God's revelation was a gift: unearned, undeserved, unexpected. In his zeal for the law, Paul had expressed his desire to serve the God of Israel, but he had no inkling of the new direction that service was to take. Without apparent warning God revealed his Jesus Christ to Paul as Son.

Paul does not say how the revelation happened. Did he see a vision or hear a voice? Did the revelation include images? Paul is content to say that he came to know Jesus Christ, and that this revelation enabled him to find meaning in his life. It began to create a new story about how God planned to save the world in and through Jesus Christ. That story would yield new values to be embodied in new social patterns and actions.

God's revelation included the call to preach Jesus Christ among the Gentiles. Paul's zealous dedication to the law gave way to preaching the good news about Jesus Christ and organizing communities of believers. Paul stresses the fact that he did not immediately go to the apostolic community in Jerusalem. He went instead to "Arabia," perhaps the area north and west of Judea, where he might have founded small communities of Christians. Paul stresses his independence to show that he first received his gospel not from the apostolic community but in a direct revelation from God.

Paul also speaks about his experience of the risen Lord in his first letter to the Corinthians: "Last of all, as to one untimely born, he (Christ) appeared also to me" (15:8). The same Lord, who had died for our sins and was buried, who was raised from the dead and appeared to Peter and the twelve, appeared to Paul. The Lord also appeared to more than five hundred persons, then to James and all the other apostles. Paul did not know Jesus during his life on earth, as did the other apostles. But he is just as much an apostle as they are because he too has seen the risen Lord. He may be the least of the apostles, since he persecuted the Church in Jerusalem. But since the risen Lord appeared to him, he can be called an apostle of Jesus Christ. It is God's gift: "... by the grace of God I am what I am, and his grace toward me was not in vain" (1 Corinthians 15:10).

In the same letter Paul asks rhetorical questions:

> Am I not free? Am I not an apostle? Have I not seen
> the Lord? Are not you my workmanship in the Lord? If
> to others I am not an apostle, at least I am to you; for
> you are the seal of my apostleship in the Lord (9:1-2).

Paul again claims his right to be an apostle, since he saw the risen
Lord. The community itself proves that God commissioned Paul to
preach Christ Jesus to the Gentiles. They experienced in his words and
actions the power that he had received from God. How could they ever
challenge his authority as an apostle of Jesus Christ?

To describe his experience Paul says that God revealed Jesus Christ
to him as Son, that the risen Lord appeared to him, and that he saw
the Lord. But he never tells us how any of this happened. Luke gives a
more detailed story: from heaven light flashed about Paul, and he fell to
the ground. Paul heard a voice: "Saul, Saul, why do you persecute me?"
... "Who are you, Lord?" ... "I am Jesus, whom you are persecuting. But
rise and enter the city, and you will be told what you are to do" (Acts
9:4-6). Luke's description satisfies his imagination and ours. But we
must not let the evangelist's account overshadow Paul's more meager
description.

When Paul wrote to the Philippians, he told them what his
experience of the risen Lord had come to mean and how it had
changed his life.

> If any other man thinks he has reason for confidence
> in the flesh, I have more: circumcised on the eighth
> day, of the people of Israel, of the tribe of Benjamin, a
> Hebrew born of Hebrews, as to the law a Pharisee, as
> to zeal persecuting the church, and to righteousness
> under the law blameless. But whatever assets were mine,
> these I have counted as loss for the sake of Christ.
> Indeed I count everything as loss because of the sur-
> passing greatness of knowing Christ Jesus my Lord.
> For his sake I have suffered the loss of all things and
> count them as refuse, that I may gain Christ and be
> found in him, not having a righteousness of my own
> based on law but that which is through faith in Christ,
> the righteousness from God that depends on faith; that
> I may know him and the power of his resurrection and
> may share his sufferings, becoming like him in his

death, that somehow I may attain the resurrection from
the dead (3:4b-11).

Paul first recalls how, like all Jewish boys, he had been initiated into the
law through circumcision. He then names with pride his Jewish roots:
people of Israel, tribe of Benjamin, Hebrew born of Hebrews. Next he
lists his achievements as a Pharisee, as a persecutor of Christians, and
as blameless under the law. Such was his life before he experienced the
risen Lord.

With a metaphor from financial bookkeeping, Paul indicates what
that experience meant to him. Assets appear in one column on a ledger,
and losses in another column. Before he experienced the risen Lord,
Paul had listed his Jewish roots and his achievements as a Pharisee in
the column marked assets. But afterward he erased "assets" and wrote
in "losses" over the same column of achievements. Knowing Christ Jesus
as his Lord had turned Paul's life upside down. That knowledge was
given to him through personal experience. It included a deep, even
mystical, fellowship with Christ's death and resurrection. With this new
perspective, Paul longed for a deeper union with Christ. He desired to
gain Christ, to be found in Christ.

Through works of the law, Paul had formerly achieved righteousness
before God, but now that righteousness came as a pure gift—a gift Paul
received through faith. With Jesus Christ at the center of his life, Paul
learned to let go of his own power, so that he might live by God's power,
which was available in that same Jesus Christ. His view of life included
union with Christ crucified and risen, righteousness by faith, and hope
in the future resurrection. In his letter to the Philippians, Paul gives us
his best account of how a new center and new values permeated his life
when he came to know Jesus Christ.

With his new dedication to Jesus Christ and his determination to
preach him to the Gentiles, Paul began a career that would include
success and failure, harmony and conflict, acceptance and rejection,
tranquility and crises. He shared Christ's sufferings and experienced
the power of his resurrection. Many Jews, especially his fellow Pharisees,
considered Paul a traitor, who had abandoned the law for the Christian
view of Jesus as the Messiah. Within the Christian movement, many
mistrusted Paul, since he had persecuted them with such cruelty and
enthusiasm. They challenged his claim to be an apostle, since he did
not know Jesus on earth.

Paul had spent his youth in the complex world of diaspora Judaism.
He had enjoyed the prestige of his position as a Pharisee in Jerusalem.
But Paul welcomed God's breaking into his life to shatter these familiar

patterns. Defining himself as an apostle of Jesus Christ, he dedicated himself to preaching the Gospel to the Gentiles. He struggled with those who would prevent him from carrying out that mission. He was not afraid to put his life on the line for his message about Jesus as Christ and Lord.

Can we interact with Paul's experience of the risen Lord? If so, how? Reflecting on swimming and floating has helped me enter into the dialogue. For Paul's transition from works of the law to faith in Jesus Christ can be compared to the transition from swimming in an indoor pool to floating on a lake.

When we swim in a pool, we set our own course and remain in charge of it. We choose the lane we want, decide how far we want to swim, and swim at the pace we want to maintain. As we swim, we keep an eye on the line at the bottom of the pool so as not to lose our course. We keep an eye out for swimmers who might wander into our lane. Having covered the distance we set for ourselves, we climb out of the pool with a sense of achievement. We have accomplished what we set out to do.

Wasn't Paul the Pharisee a swimmer in full charge of his life with God? The law was his way to God. He observed it to the best of his ability. At all times he remained in control. Achievements according to the law made him feel good about God and himself, just as swimming laps makes us feel good about ourselves.

Floating on a lake can be difficult. Although it doesn't require much skill, it does demand our letting go. Floating means learning not to do all the things we instinctively want to do. We want to keep ourselves rigid, ready to save ourselves the moment a big wave comes along. Yet the more rigid we are, the more likely we are to be swamped by the wave. Only if we relax in the water can we be carried up and over the rolling wave without sinking.

Instinctively we want to keep our heads out of the water to avoid having our nose and mouth flooded. But the more we raise our heads, the more likely we are to end up with a mouthful of water. We must persuade ourselves to put our heads back, to rest on the water as on a pillow, and to trust that we will float and not sink. Once we have discovered how to float, we never find it difficult. In fact it seems so easy that we cannot imagine why learning to relax took us so long. We are at ease in the water and at home with its movement.

After experiencing the risen Lord, Paul began to float more and swim less. He received that experience as a gift and responded to it with faith. He had neither achieved nor deserved it. He had no control over it. In trust he accepted God's gift, letting its power transform him.

He surrendered control over his relationship with God. He let himself be carried by a power other than his own. As he later said: "I have been crucified with Christ; it is no longer I who live, but Christ who lives in me; and the life I now live in the flesh I live by faith in the Son of God, who loved me and gave himself for me" (Gal 2:19b-20).

Another analogy that helps me dialogue with Paul's experience is the difference between driving an automobile or taking a bus. Imagine that we have decided to take a hundred-mile trip. If we choose to drive, we control the time we leave, the route we travel, the speed at which we drive, the number of stops we make along the way, and our time of arrival. Such control makes us feel powerful as we take our trip.

If we take a bus, we must leave at the scheduled time and follow the route determined by the bus company. We surrender control to the driver who sets the speed and determines the number of stops. We arrive at the scheduled time. In return we can sit back and enjoy the trip. We can take in the scenery or carry on a leisurely conversation. We can take a rest or read a book. We arrive relaxed at our destination.

In his experience of the risen Lord Paul learned to drive less and take more buses. He let go of the control he had enjoyed as a Pharisee and entrusted himself to God's love. He began to live by the power revealed in Christ crucified and risen.

Paul seems to have experienced this transition in an instant or at least in a short period of time. Few of us may ever experience such a sudden, unexpected, dramatic transition. Paul does not tell us what may have led up to it, and our attempts to reconstruct the process can never be more than learned conjecture. He only tells us that God revealed his Son, that the risen Lord appeared to him, and that he saw the Lord. From that moment Jesus Christ was the center of his life, faith was his highest value, and his call was to the Gentiles.

Paul's experience may seem so distant and unique that we might hesitate to dialogue with it. Certainly, to consider his experience the norm by which we judge our experiences would be a serious mistake. Over many years, however, we may undergo an adult transition that resembles Paul's in its inner dynamics. Like Paul, we may experience God challenging us to swim less and float more, to leave our car at home and take more buses. For central to Paul's experience and ours might be the invitation to change the style in which we exercise control over ourselves, over relationships in our lives, and over our relationship with God.

Control gives us the sense of being strong, of mastery, of being in charge, of power over ourselves and others. It gave the same to Paul the Pharisee. In an adult transition events in both our inner and outer worlds make maintaining this control no longer possible. In fact, we feel out of control. We see how futile has been our effort to control the outer reality of our lives and our inner reactions. As control begins to slip away, as we can no longer regulate the things that cause us pain and joy, we may panic.

In this transition God may be breaking into our lives, as he broke into Paul's, to teach us how to float more and take more buses, how to trust the gift of his love. God does not invite us to lose control but to change the style of control, to be controlled by his love. Dialoguing with Paul in his experience of the risen Lord can help us articulate the movements in our normal adult transitions, and it can lead us to live more by the power of God's love in Jesus Christ.

Perhaps you would like to stop for a moment and ask yourself some questions regarding Paul and yourself and the experience of the risen Lord:

■ How important has control been in your life? Why?
■ Have you felt that you could make yourself perfect for God? What did that feeling give you?
■ What image comes to your mind when you think of controlling and letting go?
■ How does floating in the assurance of God's love in Christ Jesus feel?
■ How has God broken into your life, shattered your control, and invited you to greater trust?

3

Missionary to the Gentiles and Community Organizer

Paul's missionary activity may have begun when he went off to found communities in Arabia. But as recounted in Acts, it began when the Holy Spirit said to the prophets and teachers in Antioch: "Set apart for me Barnabas and Saul for the work to which I have called them" (Acts 13:2). Antioch was an important city in the Roman province of Syria. Fugitives from the persecution in Jerusalem founded the Christian community in Antioch, and it soon became second only to the apostolic community in Jerusalem. As its views about membership and observances were wider than those in Jerusalem, it was probably the first community to welcome Gentile members. In Antioch the followers of Jesus were first called Christians. They also gathered a generous collection for the poorer community in Jerusalem.

Paul made Antioch his home base for his mission to the Gentiles. The community sent Barnabas and Paul on their first missionary journey: they would preach the more inclusive Christianity to Jews and Gentiles in the cities of Asia Minor. When they returned, they would report the results only to the community in Antioch.

With the community's blessing, Paul, Barnabas, and John Mark, Barnabas' cousin, departed from Seleucia, the port of Antioch. Sailing for Cyprus, they passed through the islands from Salamis to Paphos. (See map.) At Paphos, Paul made an important convert, the Roman proconsul Sergius Paulus (Acts 13:7-12). The missionaries then set sail to Perga in Pamphylia on the southern coast of central Asia Minor. Paul experienced great disappointment when John Mark deserted them to return to Jerusalem.

Paul and Barnabas moved inland to Pisidian Antioch, Iconium, Lystra, and Derbe. In Pisidian Antioch (not to be confused with their home base, Antioch in Syria), Paul preached first in the Jewish synagogue. When the Jews openly resisted him, he declared his intention to turn to the Gentiles (Acts 13:44-52). Paul and Barnabas continued

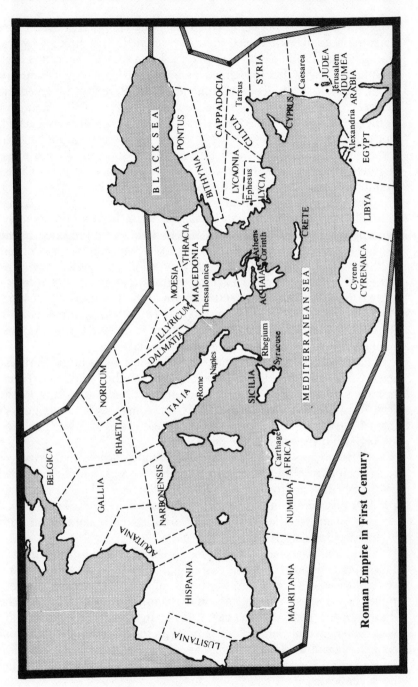

Roman Empire in First Century

to preach the Gospel, but more of their fellow Jews rejected than accepted their message. They retraced their steps from Derbe through Lystra, Iconium, and Pisidian Antioch to Perga. From Attalia they sailed back to Antioch in Syria. Paul remained there with the Christian community.

On this *first missionary journey* Paul and Barnabas preached the Gospel of Jesus Christ to Jews and Gentiles. In each city they went first to the Jewish synagogue. As Jews, they knew they would be welcomed. But when their fellow Jews refused to hear their message, they moved away from the synagogue and turned to the Gentiles. This strategy reflected their conviction that God planned salvation in Jesus Christ first for the Jews, then for the Gentiles.

Diaspora synagogues were home for the Jews away from their homeland. But Gentiles interested in Judaism also attached themselves to the synagogues. In their travels Paul and Barnabas first preached in the synagogues and then organized communities apart from the synagogues. With the community established they moved on to another town. The pattern that emerged was preaching in the synagogue, initial interest, increasing hostility, open rejection, move to the Gentiles—in Pisidian Antioch (Acts 13:13-52), in Iconium (Acts 14:1-7), in Lystra (Acts 14:8-20). Paul would experience the same pattern on later journeys, until his final confrontation with Jews in Rome (Acts 28:17-28).

Paul's success with the Gentiles raised critical issues in the Christian movement. Must Gentiles become Jews to be Christians? Must they imitate Christian Jews in being circumcised and submitting to the Jewish law? Must they observe the sabbath? Must they follow the Jewish dietary customs? Christians at Antioch were deeply divided. Paul and Barnabas returned to face the dissension.

Christian Jews with a Pharisaic background had come from Jerusalem to Antioch to teach that salvation for both Jews and Gentiles depended on their being circumcised and observing the Jewish law. In response, the Antioch community sent Paul and Barnabas to Jerusalem to seek a decision about whether salvation depended on faith alone or on faith with observance of the law.

Paul and Barnabas met with the Jerusalem community. Christian Pharisees continued to insist that Gentiles must be circumcised and observe the law. A conflict arose when Paul and Barnabas defended the rights of Gentiles. The apostles and elders intervened to resolve the disagreement. Peter won the day with the argument that circumcision was not required of Gentile Christians. With that decision, the Jerusalem council opened the Christian movement equally to Jews and Gentiles. Paul's radical view that in Christ there was neither Jew nor Greek had been vindicated.

Paul returned to Antioch, and Peter soon came to visit. At first both Peter and Paul ate with Gentile Christians in their homes and ignored the Jewish dietary customs that forbade such contact between Jews and Gentiles. A short time later, however, Christian Pharisees came from Jerusalem and began to criticize Peter for eating with Gentiles. Peter yielded to their censure and stopped. Other Christian Jews followed Peter's example so that even Barnabas no longer ate in Gentile homes. Paul challenged Peter. He showed him how he was violating his own principles by not "walking straight according to the truth of the Gospel" (Gal 2:14). Paul seems to have made his point with Peter.

Whether Gentile Christians should observe or not observe the law would continue to obstruct Paul's missionary work until it was resolved in a letter from James, the leader in Jerusalem. He stated that Gentile Christians were to abstain at least from meat sacrificed to idols, from blood, from the meat of strangled animals, and from illicit sexual union (Acts 15:22-29).

Silas accompanied Paul on his *second missionary journey*. (See map.) From Antioch they made their way through Syria and Cilicia to the towns of Derbe and Lystra. In Lystra Paul welcomed Timothy as his trusted companion. He then passed through Phrygia to Galatia. He continued to preach the Gospel and establish Christian communities. When he was prevented from proceeding to Bithynia, Paul moved on to Mysia and Troas where Luke joined him as a co-worker.

A dream-vision indicated that Paul should pass over to Neapolis, the port of Philippi, where he established the first Christian community in Europe. After he was imprisoned and flogged for exorcising a slave girl, he proceeded to Thessalonica. During his short stay he preached his Gospel and argued with Jews who incited the crowds against him. Paul fled to Beroea, and from Beroea he moved on to Athens. Paul tried to win the Athenians to the risen Jesus, but he failed to hold their attention (Acts 17:22-32).

Next Paul moved to Corinth, a most important port-city in the Mediterranean world. In Corinth he lived with Aquila and Priscilla, Jewish Christians, whom the emperor Claudius had recently expelled from Rome. From them Paul would have learned about the Christian community in Rome. He would later send this community one of his most important letters.

In Corinth, Paul departed from his usual custom and stayed for eighteen months. He won many Jews and Gentiles to his Gospel. He founded a predominantly Gentile Christian community. From Corinth Paul also wrote his first two letters to the community at Thessalonica.

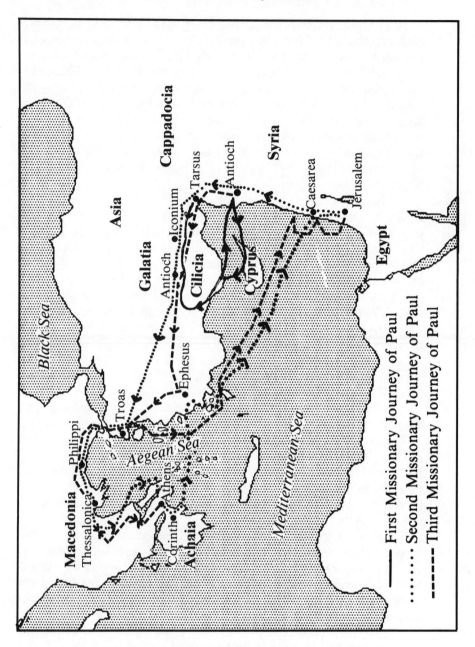

Jewish opponents began to attack Paul. They dragged him before the Roman proconsul Gallio, accusing him of "persuading men to worship God contrary to the law" (Acts 18:13). Gallio refused to pass judgment and dismissed the case against Paul. Soon afterward Paul left Corinth for Ephesus and sailed from there to Caesarea Maritima. After visiting the Jerusalem community, Paul returned home to Antioch where he stayed for more than a year.

Paul wrote most of his letters on his *third missionary journey*. (See map.) From Antioch he traveled overland to Ephesus, the capital of Asia. Ephesus was the center of his missionary activity for three years. Soon after his arrival, Paul wrote a letter to the churches of Galatia (circa CE 54), and later he wrote most likely from prison to the community at Philippi (circa CE 56).

Paul also heard that the Corinthian church was riddled with doubts, factions, scandals, and resentment against him. A period of intense communication followed in which Paul wrote at least four letters to Corinth, not all of which survive. In a first letter he warned the Corinthian community about associating with immoral men in their port-city. Shortly before Pentecost CE 55 he responded to the reports and questions that he had received by writing what we know as First Corinthians. The community did not accept his letter with total enthusiasm. Other Christian missionaries challenged Paul's claim to be an apostle and tried to discredit his message.

Relations between Paul and the Corinthians continued to deteriorate. A hasty trip to Corinth only escalated the crisis. Back in Ephesus Paul wrote a letter which he described as written "with many tears" (2 Cor 2:3-4). He sent it with Titus to Corinth as an appeal for reconciliation. Meanwhile, enemies in Ephesus protested against Paul and the spread of Christianity. Paul left Ephesus for Macedonia, where Titus returned from Corinth to meet him. Titus informed Paul that reconciliation with the Corinthians had begun to happen. So Paul wrote Second Corinthians to continue the healing. He also determined soon to make a third visit to Corinth.

Paul also began planning for the future. First he would return to Jerusalem with a collection for the poor. He had agreed with the leaders in Jerusalem to be mindful of the poor Christians in Palestine. He had asked his Gentile communities in Galatia, Macedonia, and Achaia to gather money, which he would now take to Jerusalem. His visit would also mark the end of his activity in the eastern Mediterranean. From Jerusalem he would sail to Rome, and from Rome he would move westward to Spain to complete his work of preaching Jesus Christ to the Gentile world. In anticipation of his visit, Paul wrote to the Christians in Rome.

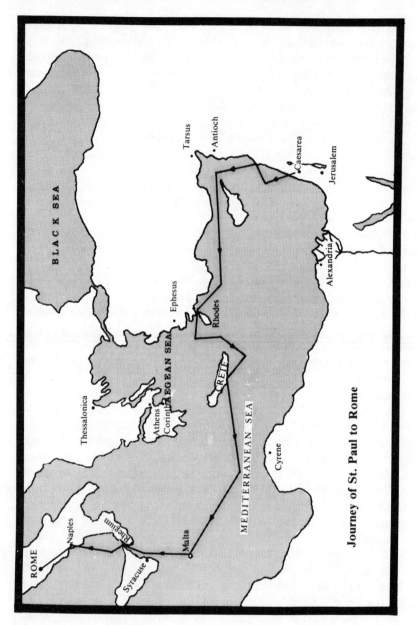

Journey of St. Paul to Rome

This letter was probably written from Corinth at the beginning of CE 58.

When spring came, Paul planned to sail from Corinth to Syria. But when some Jews plotted against him, he resolved to travel overland through Macedonia. Co-workers from Beroea, Thessalonica, Derbe, and Ephesus accompanied Paul with the collection. After Passover in Philippi, Paul left by ship for Troas, journeyed overland to Assos, and set sail for Mitylene. Skirting the coast of Asia Minor, Paul sailed from Chios to Samos, then to Miletus where he addressed the elders of the Christian community in Ephesus (Acts 20:17-35). Their prediction of his coming imprisonment did not deter Paul. He sailed on to Cos, Rhodes, Patara in Lycia, Tyre in Phoenicia, Ptolemais, and Caesarea Maritima. An overland journey brought him to Jerusalem, which he expected to reach in time for Pentecost (CE 58).

When Jesus Christ became the center of his life, Paul responded to God's call to make him known to the Gentiles. His missionary journeys reveal Paul the activist, the missionary on the move, the community organizer. As missionary and organizer, Paul deepened what he had come to know in his experience of the risen Lord. His own successes and failures, his joys and disappointments, as well as the struggles in the communities he founded, enabled Paul to develop the comprehensive view of the Christian life that we find in his letters. His call from God was to Jews and Gentiles throughout the Mediterranean world. His tasks were to preach the Gospel and establish communities. Others could tend to their growth and development.

How did Paul carry out these tasks? He depended on a team of missionary-organizers. Co-workers such as Silvanus, Timothy, Titus, Barnabas, Sosthenes, Phoebe, Junia, and others. These co-workers were essential to Paul's mission. Titus, for example, was more effective than Paul in raising funds for the Christians in Palestine. Paul's co-workers carried his letters to different communities. He always wrote on behalf of those who had labored with him and included greetings from those with him as he wrote.

Paul and his co-workers divided their work. Paul did regularly baptize and must have left this important work to others. Paul preached his Gospel. He instructed the young communities about how they were to live in accord with that preaching. He was the chief teacher-trainer on the missionary team, but he left other concerns to his companions.

Paul followed a fixed itinerary. In an orderly way he worked "from Jerusalem as far around as Illyricum" (Rom 15:19), that is, around the Mediterranean coastline to the Adriatic. He stayed in one place only long enough to establish the Gospel and organize a house-based community. After twenty years of struggle, Paul in his mid-fifties was planning the next phase of his mission, a journey to Rome and then westward to Spain.

Paul organized communities through demonstrations of power in word and action. He supported himself in most places. He successfully reached the people in Galatia, but he approached the Corinthians with fear and weakness. Hardship and suffering made him all the more loyal to the communities he founded. He expected those communities to be equally loyal to him and to his Gospel.

Paul remained open, flexible, and pragmatic about cultural differences. Paul the Pharisee had rigorously observed the law with its cultic and dietary customs. As missionary to the Gentiles, he declared these customs no longer important. Paul could eat non-kosher food with Gentiles in Antioch, and still follow Jewish customs in Jerusalem. What mattered was his mission to the Gentiles. All else had value in relation to that mission: "I have become all things to all people, so that I might save some by whatever means" (1 Cor 9:22).

Women were among Paul's co-workers. Paul never had to defend the right of women to participate in his work. Women as well as men were leaders in his communities. Women appear alongside men in Paul's greetings to and from his co-workers. In his letter to the Philippians he singles out two women leaders who were at odds with each other. He emphasizes that "they have labored side-by-side with me in the Gospel" (Phil 4:2-3). When women's leadership became an issue in Corinth, all sides in the dispute assumed that women could lead worship (1 Cor 11:2-16).

Paul's missionary strategy and style were rooted in the fact that God had called him to be an apostle to the Gentiles. Paul strove to proclaim his Gospel to the entire world—through Asia Minor, Macedonia, Greece, Rome, and Spain. He enlisted men and women co-workers to travel with him, and they may have lived in community. As he and his companions moved from place to place, their first priority was to preach the Gospel, to organize house-based communities, and to nurture them for a time. They would then move on to repeat the same activities in the next city. They lived vulnerable, risk-filled lives. They frequently faced misunderstanding and hostility.

Can we dialogue with Paul's strategy and style for the Gentile mission? We must first recall a significant difference. Paul and his co-workers were the first missionaries to the Gentile world, whereas we live in a Church with established offices and traditions. We cannot forget the distance in time and the differences in culture that separate us from Paul.

Yet Christianity has begun a transition that resembles the transition that took place in the early Christian movement because of Paul's mission to the Gentiles. It has begun to change from a European religion to a world religion. Europe and America no longer control a Christianity that was exported to Asia and Africa. Third world countries with their rich cultures now shape local customs and practices that no longer depend on the west.

This change resembles what happened when Paul preached Jesus Christ to the Gentile world. His activities transformed a Christianity that had been exclusively Jewish into a movement in which the distinction between Jews and Gentiles lost all meaning. When Paul declared circumcision unnecessary for Gentiles, Christianity began to take root and grow on pagan soil and be deeply informed by Hellenistic culture. Today we share in a similar transition, as the Christianity of Europe and America gives way to a religion rooted and growing in all cultures, east and west, first and third worlds.

Such radical transitions raise questions and often introduce conflict. Paul asked whether Gentiles must become Jews to be Christians. We ask whether Asians and Africans must become Westerners to be Christians. Paul asked whether Gentiles must observe prescriptions about the sabbath and customs about eating. We ask whether Christians in Asia and Africa must worship according to western liturgical forms instead of creating new forms out of their own culture. Such questions divided the Christian movement in its earliest days, as they divide the Church today. Christian Pharisees insisted that Gentiles be circumcised and observe the law. Paul and Barnabas responded that faith alone sufficed for both Jews and Gentiles. For in Christ there was neither Jew nor Greek.

Different understandings of Church renewal currently struggle with each other in parish meetings, in schools, in diocesan synods, in religious and lay communities, even in international headquarters. Should we Christians actively participate in economic, social, and political issues at the national and world level? Or do such issues have no place in our churches? Shall we ordain women and homosexual men? Or are they forever excluded from ordained ministry? New patterns have begun to emerge in the Christian churches that in the long run will change how we think, feel, and act. Can we learn from Paul's missionary activity, from his style and strategy? I think we can.

In the Catholic Church, for example, we are facing a gradual, but decisive decline in the number of ordained priests and vowed religious. At the same time we are growing significantly in the number of non-ordained lay leaders and ministers. We have traditionally considered priesthood and religious life a higher calling than marriage, but now married people have begun to share in almost all aspects of the Church ministry.

As women's gifts become needed and recognized, male supremacy is declining in the Church. Clerics no longer monopolize power, as lay people are given ministerial and financial responsibilities formerly reserved to priests. In the future, the shortage of priests will make the Eucharist less available to the people. Lay persons will assume more responsibility in preaching, teaching, and witnessing to the word of God.

Paul and his co-workers preached the Gospel, organized house-based communities, nurtured them for a while, and then moved on to the next city. We live in stable organizations called parishes. From that base we minister to fellow parishioners, to people in our neighborhoods, and to cities and the world. Our ministries include liturgy, preaching, religious education, and social services. In carrying them out might we not imitate Paul's zeal and dedication? Might we not develop teams of co-workers, men and women, to share decision-making and responsibilities? Might we not support each other in both the joys and struggles of ministry, in our successes and failures, in the misunderstandings and conflicts? I suggest that in spite of clear differences Paul can contribute to how we go about ministry in this time of deep transition.

Paul experienced much conflict as he participated in the transition in which the distinction between Jew and Gentile lost all meaning. Conflict is a fact in the Church today. We all feel the tension it produces. We may want to run from the pain, whether back to the past or simply away from the present. Retrenchment and discouragement, however, both fail to recognize that the Holy Spirit might be speaking to the Church in and through the conflict.

Historical circumstances forced Paul and his fellow Christians to face deep identity questions for which there were no easy, clear-cut answers. As we become a world Church, we face similar questions and wait patiently for answers to emerge. Paul teaches us that conflicts can lead to growth. He invites us to live with the tension, even welcome it. For without conflict the Christian movement might never have moved out from Judaism to the Gentile world. Paul encourages us to accept our confusion, even though we may not like it. He invites us to live with present ambiguities and uncertainties about the future. Finally, he urges us to remain fearless in our choice of Christ and the Church.

Let's reflect for a few moments on this chapter and perhaps dialogue with Paul, missionary to the Gentiles and community organizer.

■ Is your ministry like Paul's in any way?

- What changes and conflicts do you see happening in the Church? Are these perhaps of the Holy Spirit? Why or why not?
- What adjectives come to your mind now when you think of Paul as a missionary?
- What talents and skills do you have to bring to a world Church?
- What do you learn from Paul—what images, what words—about change?
- What else occurs to you?

4

Letter Writer

Writing letters was a popular practice in the Hellenistic world. Paul introduced it into the Christian movement. Did Paul write letters merely to communicate with distant communities? Did he intend his letters to be personal and confidential or destined for a wider Christian audience? Did he mean them to apply more widely than to the particular situation he addressed?

Paul pioneered the letter as a means to communicate with the communities that he had founded in Asia Minor and Greece. In them he blended experience, traditions, and culture. Experience included his coming to know the risen Lord, what he learned from his activities as missionary and community organizer, and his concrete relationship to the community he addressed. He incorporated traditions that he continued to cherish as a Jew, as well as traditions he had come to value as a Christian. Finally the Greco-Roman culture informed his letters, since it was Paul's from his childhood and also that of his communities. Information from these three sources merged in the process Paul used in writing his letters. The following diagram may help us visualize that process.

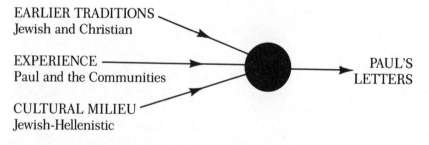

EARLIER TRADITIONS
Jewish and Christian

EXPERIENCE
Paul and the Communities

CULTURAL MILIEU
Jewish-Hellenistic

PAUL'S
LETTERS

We have described how Paul wrote most of his letters on his third missionary journey. In them he addressed the complex problems and relationships that surfaced in the young Christian communities. Their members accepted his Gospel about Jesus Christ and were baptized. More often than not, however, they did not know how to live as Christians both within the community and in relation to the surrounding Hellenistic culture. Paul wrote his letters to maintain good relations with these communities or reestablish them if they had been broken. But he was primarily concerned to show the new Christians the deeper meaning of their faith and how they should live in the light of that faith. At times that concern led him to risk creating further antagonism toward him and conflict within the community.

Paul sought information about the concrete situation of the community, and he described for his readers the setting from which he wrote. Those who carried his letters gave the communities news about Paul. But in his letters Paul did not hide his feelings about their situation. He responded to the information that he had received, and he told them how he saw the Gospel that he had preached at work in their everyday lives. Paul did not so much forge doctrine, as help his struggling communities live out their commitment to Jesus Christ.

Paul wrote as an apostle of Jesus Christ, that is, with the authority that came from having seen the risen Lord and from having worked as a missionary to the Gentiles. Sensitive about his right to be an apostle, Paul defended himself with vigor when others attacked. He asked respect and obedience from the communities that he had founded. In return, he demonstrated unconditional loyalty and fidelity. He knew that his mission was rooted in God, and his communities were a proof of its authenticity.

Paul's letters never replaced his personal presence. In fact he often reminded his communities that he would much rather see them face-to-face than communicate through letters. He remained open to future visits. Even at a distance, however, Paul advised them on specific issues and questions. His letters, which expressed what Paul would have said in person if he had been with the community, can hardly be considered literary masterpieces.

Paul sent his letters with trusted carriers, who delivered them and expanded on their contents. Since his letters did not exhaust all that he wanted to say, his co-workers gave fuller explanations and made practical applications. The letters carried Paul's message in its essentials and provided a basis for further development. When they were read in community, the co-workers explained the letters and responded to questions.

About ten years after their composition, Paul's letters were probably collected. Initially, Paul wrote to individual communities who were distant from each other. At first the letter was read aloud in that assembly. Eventually, it was read in the community's more formal liturgies. Later, the letters may have been collected to serve such liturgical needs or because other communities needed teaching and practical advice from someone as significant as Paul.

When later generations faced dissension and conflict, Paul's letters might have enabled them to recapture the founding spirit of the community. Also, after his death Paul came to be honored as the great missionary to the Gentiles. His letters were recognized as written not only to the communities addressed but also to Christians in every age and situation.

Literary Form

Reading Paul's letters is very different from reading the Gospels. An analogy may explain what the reader must do. Imagine a mother waiting for her children to come downstairs for breakfast. Without thinking she prepares herself differently to receive each child. She knows each child in his or her unique personality and instinctively receives each one according to his or her temperament.

Reading Gospels and letters is also like a shortstop in baseball who prepares differently to field different kinds of balls. For a grounder a shortstop bends over so as to scoop up the ball and throw to first base in time to get the runner. For a line drive the same shortstop stands, jumps, or dives to catch the hard-hit ball before it gets through to the outfield. For a fly ball, the shortstop follows it into the sun, tries not to lose it in the glare, and holds two hands like a basket to catch it.

Paul's letters come at us, as we read them, in a way that differs greatly from the Gospels. Letters and Gospels are like different children in a family or different balls coming at a shortstop. We must set ourselves to receive letters differently from a Gospel. Gospels tell a tale about Jesus of Nazareth, and we receive them as a story with plot, characterization, and dramatic movement. In his letters, Paul makes statements about God's action in Jesus Christ and instructs his communities about how they are to live. If we expect to find a tale in Paul's letters, we will be frustrated and disappointed. We will not receive his letters as letters, nor will we find meaning in his message.

Setting ourselves to receive Paul's letters means reflecting on their literary form. A letter of sympathy is a contemporary letter form. It arises out of the actual situation that someone significant to us has died. We all write to the same person. If we were to look at all the letters, we would find that all of us have more or less said the same things. We all described our surprise at hearing of the death. We all expressed our sympathy to the bereaved. Most of us recalled a fond memory of the deceased. We all assured our friend that we would continue to support him or her with our prayers. These sentiments constitute a letter of sympathy. While we may use different words to express these sentiments and arrange them in different sequences, we all include them in our letters because they express what is proper to this situation.

The concrete situation, as well as the contemporary style of writing letters, determined the literary form of Paul's letters. Six elements normally appear in the identical sequence: address, greeting, thanksgiving, message, final greeting, benediction. None of these elements occur in a Gospel. Becoming sensitive to these six components will enable us to receive Paul's letters as letters.

In the *address* Paul introduces himself as the sender, mentions his co-senders, and names those to whom the letter is written. How he describes himself sets a tone for the letter. For example, he introduces himself to the Galatians as "an apostle not from men nor through man, but through Jesus Christ and God the Father, who raised him from the dead" (Gal 1:1). We suspect that an issue about Paul's authority might have occasioned this letter. Paul introduces himself to Philemon as "a prisoner for Christ Jesus" (Phlm 1:1). He sets a much more intimate, mutual tone of affection.

Normally, Paul refers to his apostolic authority to establish his credentials. As an apostle, he is entitled to address the community, admonish its members, and help it resolve its difficulties. Paul also mentions his co-workers as trusted persons who will deliver the letter and further elaborate on its contents. He expects the community to acknowledge their authority. Paul often mentions the special status of the community as recipients of the good news, as holy ones and saints, as the church in that region.

In *greeting* the community, Paul uses the same basic formula: "Grace and peace be yours from God our Father and the Lord Jesus Christ" (2 Thes 1:2). Sometimes Paul expands the greeting with words or phrases about God the Father and Jesus Christ. Frequently the solemnity of this greeting suggests that Paul may have adapted it from a popular formula used in the Christian liturgy. With it Paul sends his readers the "grace" and "peace" available to them in this messianic age through Jesus Christ their Lord.

In the *thanksgiving* Paul discloses the reason for the letter, its dominant themes, and his attitude toward the community addressed. He provides valuable insights into his life and personality. In First Thessalonians he devotes almost three-fifths of the letter to thanksgiving, and in Second Corinthians he develops the thanksgiving into an extended blessing (2 Cor 1:3-11). Paul gives thanks for the success of the community and prays that their success may continue. For success means that God's power is at work in them. Paul often combines his gratitude for the present with a vision of God's final power being revealed over all creation. In his letter to the Galatians, Paul substitutes an angry rebuke for his customary thanksgiving (Gal 1:6-9).

In each letter's *message* Paul speaks to the particular issues that bring him to write this community at this time. Without any set pattern he adapts his content and style to what the situation demands. Within this great variety, however, Paul models his message on his preaching. For he generally moves from statements about God's action in Jesus Christ to exhortations and instructions about the implications of the good news for the community. Since Paul dialogues with concrete issues, we cannot expect to understand or find meaning in his message without a sense of its historical context.

In the *final greetings* Paul frequently includes news about himself and those with him, as well as advice for specific individuals in the community. He might reveal a special relationship to some member, talk about his co-workers, or send regards to particular persons. His brief remarks provide important glimpses into his travels and various activities.

Paul concludes with a simple *benediction*: "The grace of our Lord Jesus Christ be with you." This solemn closing echoes the initial greeting. It expresses Paul's prayer for the community that they continue to develop and grow in the Lord. He writes as a man of prayer and formulates his letter in a context of prayer.

Address, greeting, thanksgiving, message, final greeting, benediction —these six elements in the same sequence constitute the literary form of a Pauline letter. They determine how the letters come at us when we read them, and they suggest how we might set ourselves to receive them. It is difficult to say whether Paul wrote his letters in his own hand, dictated them word-by-word to someone else, gave the sense of his message to a co-worker who formulated the letter, or at times simply instructed a co-worker to write in his name. He may have used different methods for different letters. But Paul claimed the letters as his own. At times he added a statement in his own hand to assure the community that he was the author.

Hints for Reading

Paul often included in his letters scraps of traditional Christian preaching, material from homilies, exhortations, lists of virtues and vices, Christian hymns, formulas from the liturgy, proof-texts from the Hebrew Testament, diatribes against imagined opponents. He followed the letter form, but he filled it with varied content. Paul did not write with the precision that we find in creeds and law-codes, conciliar documents, or systematic theology. He rarely elaborated his cherished beliefs, and he expressed them in a style and language that betrays him as a man who speaks as he writes.

Paul wrote with personal eloquence and deep feelings. His letters reveal a vivid imagination and a passionate temperament. As a result, his letters are rich in symbols and metaphors that invite the reader to discover the deeper meaning in his message. If we let ourselves be drawn into those symbols and metaphors, we will gradually find that deeper level of meaning. We may grapple with the metaphors, but we should neither tear them apart with our minds nor rush to concrete application. We must let them live in us, draw us into their world, and disclose to us their reality.

Paul's metaphors point to basic human situations like building a building, conjugal union, the human body, athletes in a contest, gardeners who plant and water. Paul's central metaphors concern persons in relationship to each other—salvation, redemption, ransom, sanctification, liberation, justification, transformation, reconciliation. Paul uses metaphors insofar as they disclose the meaning of his message about God's action in Jesus Christ. At times he begins to explore one metaphor, quickly discards it for another, and ends by rejecting the second metaphor for a third. His thought seems so vigorous and his conviction so strong that metaphors seem to crack in his hand. We can be frustrated with such a rapid, jerky movement of thought.

Paul tends to present reality in terms of opposites that reflect his dualistic world view, such as old age/new age, death/life, weakness/power, folly/wisdom, flesh/spirit, already/not yet, sin/grace, unity/diversity, darkness/light, Adam/Christ, works of the law/faith in Christ Jesus. He views these polarities not so much as radical either/or dichotomies but as simultaneous both/and realities. Paul realizes that Christians live in both the new age and the old age at the same time. They are both already saved and not yet fully saved. As we read Paul's letters, we will sense how he moves between these polarities and works to keep opposites in creative tension.

Paul presents realities like sin, death, and the law as actors in the drama of salvation history. Sin entered the drama with Adam's transgression, and death entered the world through sin. Sin led to death, and death resulted from sin. Another actor, the law, was introduced at Sinai. Though holy and good, the law was co-opted by sin to lead persons to death. But when Jesus Christ died and rose from the dead, God broke this unholy alliance. Paul personifies these and other realities to draw us more vividly into his drama about God's action in Christ. We must be careful to read them as persons, not as abstract concepts.

Paul's thought often moves more in a concentric pattern than in a straight line. He states proposition A, then he adds some considerations —B—that seem to digress from what he just said, and then he returns to the original statement—A1—which the apparent digression actually supports. Paul uses this A-B-A1 movement most often in Romans. He announces the revelation of God's justice (A = 1:17). He then argues that Jews and Gentiles alike have deserved God's wrath (B = 1:18-3:20). Finally he returns to explain God's justice (A1 = 3:21-30). The long digression on sin's universal power establishes the need for God's justice in Christ to save both Jews and Greeks.

As we read Paul's letters, we do well to remember that his strong intuition often leads him to leap from principles to conclusions without care for the logical steps in-between. His feelings and imagination enabled him to develop powerful metaphors from human experience. Paul tended to present reality in both/and polarities. He considered sin, death, and the law as actors in the drama of salvation history. He tended to think more in concentric than linear patterns.

Now I invite you to read the letters that we are sure Paul himself wrote: First and Second Thessalonians, Galatians, First and Second Corinthians, Romans, Philippians, and Philemon. I suggest that you read them one at a time as letters. You might want to become more familiar with them before continuing with this book. Or you may prefer reading them along with the next section, "Finding Meaning in Paul's Message." In reading one letter at a time, you will form a distinct impression of that letter apart from the others. If possible, read each letter more than once. First, focus on the individual words, phrases, and sentences to become more aware of each element in the letter. In a second reading attend more to the sense lines and units of thought and experience the letter's texture, movement, and overall themes. Finally, watch how you respond to the letter as you read it the third time. The following questions are suggested for your reflection:

■ What three adjectives best describe the letter? What passages in the letter support each adjective?
■ What is the tone of the letter? What is the relationship between Paul and the community addressed?
■ What are the dominant themes in the letter? What words and phrases are most often repeated?
■ What aspects of the letter did you like most? What did you find meaningful? What aspects did you ignore or resist? What was your overall reaction?

We have dialogued with Paul of Tarsus—as diaspora Jew and Pharisee of the Pharisees, in his experience of the risen Lord, as missionary to the Gentiles and community organizer, and as letter writer. We have listened to Paul, the man, and learned about his situation. We have responded from our own situation. We stand apart from Paul in personality and temperament, in historical context, in background and culture, in our experience of God, and in our call to mission. But we also resemble him in a basic humanness that transcends time and culture. We have begun to see that Paul can inform and influence us across the distance in time and the differences in culture. Now we want to see what meaning we might find in his message.

Part II

FINDING MEANING IN PAUL'S MESSAGE

We all search for meaning in our lives. We want to share with others a common vision of what being human means. As human beings, we need some grasp of the larger picture in which we are situated. We look for what can give coherence to the many pieces that make up that larger picture. As humans, we are drawn to live at more than a mundane level, to see deeper dimensions, and to act in accord with them. We relate to ourselves and to our neighbors, to our surroundings and to the world, and ultimately to God. We hope that these relationships will make our lives meaningful. As humans, we value images that make sense out of our experiences. We prize symbols and metaphors that tell about our origins, give meaning to our present experience, and orient us toward the future.

Now let's reflect on how we find meaning in our lives.

- What gets your best time, your best energy?
- For what causes, dreams, goals or institutions do you pour out your life?
- What do you fear or dread most in life? What do you most rely on and trust?
- To whom or what have you committed your life? For what are you ready to give your life?
- With whom or what group do you share your most sacred and private hopes for yourself and for those you love?
- What are your most sacred hopes? What are your most compelling goals and purposes?
- What are your values, the patterns of your love and action, the shape of fear and dread in your life, the directions of hope and friendship?

How might Paul's message help us find meaning in our lives? We will explore this question by moving between what his message meant for his first century communities and what the same message might mean for us as twentieth century Christians. I invite you into Paul's drama about God's action in Jesus Christ. I encourage you to experience it with head and heart, with thought and feeling, with reason and imagination. For only through such participation will we discover how Paul's message might ground us in our religious past, help us find meaning in our present, and guide us toward the future.

Participating in Paul's message means being open and sensitive to his symbols and metaphors. We let ourselves be drawn into them and through them into contact with the deeper, hidden reality that they disclose. A symbol mediates reality, because it enables us to experience the power of the reality through some concrete form. For example, some years ago I visited a woman who was hospitalized with the final stages of a painful cancer. As we talked, I stood at the foot of her hospital bed. She asked me to move to one side or the other because I was blocking her view of the inexpensive crucifix on the wall behind me. She wanted to keep her eyes on that crucifix, since in and through that visible form she experienced the power of God's love. That power enabled her to endure pain and face death with hope, since she was convinced that nothing could separate her from the love symbolized by the crucifix. That inexpensive crucifix functioned as a symbol through which she experienced the hidden, mysterious reality of God's unconditional love.

Paul talks about that love through metaphors when he preaches "Christ crucified ... the power of God and the wisdom of God" (1 Cor 1:23-24). Literally, his words sound absurd. A crucified Messiah implies weakness not power, foolishness not wisdom. Paul's words seem ridiculous, impossible, and contradictory. No wonder both Jews and Gentiles found them difficult to accept. We too may be tempted to dismiss his words. But if we let them live in us, we may gradually find their deeper meaning.

We stay with the tension in Paul's statement. We watch its literal meaning begin to melt away. A hidden, mysterious meaning begins to spring up between phrases that at first seemed contradictory: "Christ crucified ... power ... wisdom." Resemblances begin to appear between terms that first seemed contradictory. We begin to notice that power can be found in apparent weakness, that wisdom can be learned from apparent foolishness. What the dying woman experienced by gazing at the crucifix, we begin to experience through Paul's preaching.

Through symbols and metaphors, Paul invites us into the hidden, mysterious world of God's action in Jesus Christ. He invites us to discover what meaning it might disclose. At first it may seem like a strange and foreign land, but it will gradually become a familiar, comfortable place in which we begin to feel at home. As we become more enchanted, Paul's message will disclose its power. Some elements will resonate with our experience, other elements will seem distant, still others will rub against or even shatter our world view. Our willingness to interact with Paul's message reveals an openness to let it inform and influence how we make meaning in our lives.

What is Paul's message? It concerns God's action in Jesus Christ. Paul received it in his experience of the risen Lord, and it continued to unfold in his mission to the Gentiles. He preached it throughout Asia Minor, Macedonia, and Greece. He persuaded many Jews and Gentiles. He founded communities on that message, and he reminded them of it in his letters.

We can visualize Paul's message as a drama with three scenes. Scene One, "Dying and Rising in Christ," opens onto a dark stage with a tall cross at the center. The cross alone is bathed in light, so that our attention might be drawn to it. For it is the central symbol in Paul's drama of salvation. We are invited to experience the power in its paradox. In Chapter Five we will look at this scene and reflect on how it might enable us to find meaning in apparently meaningless suffering.

Scene Two, "God's Plan of Action for the World," focuses on the men and women moving behind the cross. These persons act in the drama of God's plan for the world. We recognize Adam and Abraham, persons called sin and death, and another named the Law. As we watch them reenact the drama of salvation history, we will see how the cross at center stage is its turning point. In Chapter Six we will explore this drama and reflect on how it enabled Paul to find meaning in the conflict between God's promises to Israel and his mission to the Gentiles. We will ask what we might learn for times when we face similar conflicts.

Scene Three, "Individuals and Communities in the New Age," draws our attention to persons around the front of the cross. They are looking at both the cross and the characters behind it. Their backs are to us in the audience. These believers and faith communities have accepted Paul's message. Now they ask what their commitment might mean in their everyday lives. In Chapter Seven we will focus on what the cross affects in these individuals and communities. We will explore some of the metaphors that Paul uses and ask what power these metaphors might have in our search for meaning. We will also describe how Paul would have them and us discover the continuing action of the Spirit in our lives.

These three scenes dramatize Paul's message. I have teased them out of his letters, since Paul himself nowhere provides a synthesis of his thought. I have placed the crucified and risen Jesus at center stage, and I have arranged the other characters around that center. I could have made God's plan the center or the individuals and faith communities. But whoever describes Paul's message must include how Jesus' death and resurrection reveals God's action in the world (Scene One—Chapter Five), how that action is the turning point in salvation history (Scene Two—Chapter Six), and how persons and faith communities participate in that action (Scene Three—Chapter Seven).

5

Dying and Rising in Christ

We all experience pain in life, even though we
may not experience the same kinds of pain,
the same causes of pain, the same degree of pain. We experience pain
in different situations and for different reasons. That pain might be
physical, emotional, intellectual, psychological or spiritual. But we can
often find a solution for the pain we are experiencing. When we have a
headache, we can take medicine to get rid of it. When we are distant
from loved ones, we can reach out and touch them with a phone call to
relieve our loneliness.

At the other extreme, however, is suffering that may so overwhelm
us that we seem to lose all power and freedom to respond. People are
trapped by forces that paralyze their human freedom. In their struggle
to survive, they are unable to ask what their suffering might mean.

Suffering may also be more than a problem to be solved but less
than the pain that destroys the human spirit. An event may shatter the
world we have known and send us on a search for its meaning. It raises
questions for which immediate answers are unavailable. It seems sense-
less, useless, without purpose. But it need not deaden our power and
freedom to search for meaning. We can still recognize power at work in
our lives. We can cry out against the unfair situation and pray that it
will be changed. If we value our lives enough, we can resist the pain
that threatens to deprive our lives of meaning. Such suffering confronts
us with mystery and invites us to live with the questions it raises. It
asks us to wait in hope that its hidden meaning will one day emerge.

Ed and Helen were around thirty, married for four years, with two
children, Martha and Tim. Three years earlier Ed had one kidney
removed and the other replaced by a transplant from his mother. His
body rejected the foreign kidney. He now faced three courses of action:
a second transplant with its doubtful success, life with a dialysis machine,
or death. Out of love for his wife and children Ed chose to die. He did
not want to put them through another surgery, and he could not tolerate

being tied to a machine for the rest of his life. He died April 23, 1978. Some people did not understand his decision. A few even called it suicide.

Bill and Randy had looked forward for years to their time of retirement. Bill had succeeded well enough in his insurance business to build up some savings. With their children raised, Randy went back to teaching geography to supplement their income. As she taught about different cities and countries, she dreamed of traveling with Bill in their retirement. Retirement finally came, but with it also came a spiraling inflation. The value of their accumulated savings quickly diminished. Far from thinking about travel, Bill and Randy had to plan carefully so that their fixed income and savings could meet their living expenses. They gave up their dreams of traveling and sightseeing, and they settled down to routine life in suburban Detroit.

In these two cases an event shattered the world the persons had put together for themselves and caused them to begin a search for meaning. Death shattered the world Ed and Helen had created for themselves and their children. Inflation shattered Bill and Randy's world with its dreams for retirement. They confronted life as painful, unmanageable, empty of meaning, ambiguous, absurd, paradoxical, and profoundly mysterious. They asked whether their suffering had any meaning. Like them, we all experience pain at times without knowing why.

Western culture marshals enormous resources in a war against suffering. It holds up a life without pain and suffering, without annoyance or inconvenience, as the ideal to be sought. We are expected to be strong when we suffer, to hide our pain from others, to consider it our enemy, to work to eliminate it from life. The advertising world wants us to imagine a life without fear and need, without inconvenience or agitation, as easy to attain. As a result, we often feel ashamed and guilty when we suffer. We are often uncomfortable with others in their suffering. We know that pain and suffering, even meaningless suffering, are normal in our adult lives. But our culture does little to help us find meaning in suffering.

Can Paul help us search for meaning in apparently meaningless suffering? We will answer this question by listening to his message about the paradox of the cross and about Christ's death and resurrection. We will then let Paul teach us how faith communities can support people in their pain, how we can recognize in our suffering the paradox and pattern of Christ's death and resurrection, and how our vision of the future can enable us to find meaning in present suffering. As we are drawn into Paul's symbols and metaphors, we will discover how they might inform and influence our search for meaning.

Before moving to Paul, however, I invite you to reflect on your experience by answering the following questions.

- Have you ever experienced suffering as "meaningless"? If so, how did you respond?
- Where did you turn to find meaning?
- What concrete situations surface when you hear the phrase, "meaningless suffering"?
- Have you companioned others in their search for meaning? How did they find meaning?

Power in Weakness

> Jews demand signs and Greeks seek wisdom, but we preach Christ crucified, a stumbling block to Jews and folly to the Gentiles, but to those who are called, both Jews and Greeks, Christ the power of God and the wisdom of God. For the foolishness of God is wiser than men, and the weakness of God is stronger than men (1 Cor 1:22-25).

Paul preached the paradox of the cross, the mystery of power in apparent weakness, of wisdom in apparent foolishness. His message challenged both Jews and Greeks because it contradicted their expectations. Paul urged the Corinthian community not to forget that God called them to accept that paradox and find its truth in their own experience.

Paradox lies at the heart of Paul's message, the paradox of power in apparent weakness, wisdom in apparent foolishness. Paradox suggests an apparent contradiction, something opposed to common sense, a reversal of ordinary logic, a world upside down. It catches us unawares, shocks and startles us. For it conflicts with how we normally find meaning in our lives. Reason alone cannot explain a paradox. It invites us to view life not as unreasonable, but as beyond reason, that is, as profoundly mysterious.

Metaphor is the language of paradox. It functions as a category mistake, a calculated error, which brings together things that do not belong together in ordinary logic. Metaphors shock us at first, because they seem absurd. The initial shock creates a tension, since the literal meaning makes no sense at all. But if we let the tension work in us, we may gradually experience the literal meaning giving way to a deeper, metaphorical meaning. We may begin to see resemblances between terms that first seemed to contradict each other. As the literal meaning self-destructs, the metaphorical meaning begins to spring up between the terms. A truth that was unavailable at the literal level begins to be disclosed.

Metaphors communicate paradoxical truth. We say, "She's a jewel!" or "He's an ox!" Literally, both statements are absurd. She is a woman, and a jewel is a stone. He is a man, and an ox is an animal. But the initial shock can create a tension that leads to a hidden truth through the experience of resemblances. A jewel is precious, opaque, beautiful. She is precious, opaque, beautiful. An ox is strong, hard-working, reliable. He is strong, hard-working, reliable. Having seen these resemblances, we can say with conviction what at first seemed absurd, namely, "She *is* a jewel!" and "He *is* an ox!"

Paul preaches power in weakness and wisdom in foolishness. At first his preaching seems absurd, but through metaphors he invites us into the mystery it announces. He preaches "Christ crucified." The term Christ, the anointed one, the Messiah, designated for the Jews the man sent by God to deliver them from Roman domination. Since 67 BCE the Romans had kept them under social, economic, political, and religious oppression. The Jewish people longed for and expected a Messiah who would reestablish them as an independent, prosperous nation under God.

Paul preached that a crucified Messiah was God's answer to their prayers. Nothing could have sounded more absurd. For death by crucifixion was a punishment which the Romans reserved for slaves and bandits, for rebels and non-Jews. Roman citizens could not be crucified. Paul shocked his fellow Jews. Literally, his words seemed ridiculous and without meaning. No man put to death on the cross by the Romans could be the Messiah sent by God to lead the Jews to freedom from Roman domination. Such a man could never be the power and wisdom of God.

Most Jews found Paul's preaching a stumbling block, and they dismissed both the man and his message. In the chaos under Roman power they had remained confident that God would fulfill the promise to establish a new age of salvation. When the Messiah would come, he would reveal himself with miracles and other clear signs of power. But Paul preached a crucified Messiah as the power and wisdom of God. Jews found his words a "stumbling block." Not only at Corinth but throughout Asia Minor and Greece, Paul's own people received his preaching with suspicion and hostility.

Gentiles also found Paul's message difficult. They searched for a wise man, a teacher, who would reveal to them the knowledge hidden in God. For that experiential knowledge would save them from the hostile world and set them free from the prison that confined them. Paul preached Christ crucified as the wisdom of God. A Jew put to death by the Romans was the divine guide who showed them the way out of this world to God. Paul's preaching so conflicted with their view of wisdom that they dismissed it as foolishness. A wise man would never have let himself be crucified. He would have known how to escape such an extreme fate, and he would have revealed that knowledge to them. They failed to recognize the deeper truth that divine wisdom is paradoxical and mysterious, that it contradicts their reasonable demands.

Most Jews and Greeks dismissed Paul's preaching, since its literal meaning made no sense to them. It did not agree with their criteria for recognizing God's action in the world. But God called some of them to let Paul's message shatter their worlds and disclose the deeper truth about power and wisdom. At first Paul's words also seemed absurd and contradictory to them. But they stayed with the tension in his words and let it live in them. Resemblances began to surface between the longed-for Messiah and death by crucifixion, between apparent weakness and divine power, between evident foolishness and divine wisdom. As the literal sense gradually gave way to a deeper meaning, God's power began to seem compatible with human weakness. God's wisdom seemed able to be revealed in human foolishness. These Jews and Gentiles moved from the contradiction in a crucified Messiah to the mystery that "the foolishness of God is wiser than men, and the weakness of God is stronger than men" (1 Cor 1:25).

Reason alone cannot explain paradox. It must be learned and verified in individual and collective experience. So Paul invites the Corinthians to reflect on God's paradoxical power, as it is revealed in their weakness and in his ministering to them. Not many of them were wise according to the world's wisdom. Not many were powerful or of noble birth. Yet God chose them to confound the powerful and shame the wise in Corinth. God's power was at work in the believers' weakness.

Paul's own behavior discloses the same paradox: "I decided to know nothing among you except Jesus Christ and him crucified" (1 Cor 2:2). Paul's conduct mirrored his message: he was with them in weakness and in much fear and trembling. His manner of speaking revealed not his own eloquence but the power of God. Both Paul's personal style and the Corinthian community struck a harmonious chord with the paradox of God's power and wisdom revealed in a crucified Messiah.

Echoes of this paradox are heard when Paul describes himself as foolish, weak, and held in disrepute in comparison to the Corinthians who are wise, strong, and held in honor (1 Cor 4:10). When he discusses eating meat sacrificed to idols, Paul urges the Corinthians to modify their behavior to keep those with a weaker conscience from stumbling (1 Cor 8:7-13). He later boasts that for the sake of preaching the Gospel he became weak to the weak that he might win the weak (1 Cor 9:22). In speaking of the human body he points out how the parts that seem weaker are the more indispensable (1 Cor 12:22). In the resurrection, the body that was sown in weakness will be raised in power (1 Cor 15:43).

Later Paul's crisis with the Corinthians will lead him to boast of his weakness, because it proves that whatever power the Corinthians may have experienced in his work must be from God. Paul compares his weakness to that of a fragile clay pot: "We have this treasure in earthen vessels, to show that the transcendent power belongs to God and not to us" (2 Cor 4:7). When he prays to be freed of a thorn in the flesh, he hears God say: "My grace is sufficient for you, for my power is made perfect in weakness" (2 Cor 12:9). Paul is content with weakness. For when he is weak, then is he strong. Paul's acceptance of God's power at work in his weakness reflected the paradox he preached, "Christ crucified, the power of God and the wisdom of God" (1 Cor 1:24).

We will find meaning in this paradox when it resonates with our adult experience. For example, we may find that over certain periods we live with a strange discrepancy between our outer world and our inner world. We continue to work productively, to carry out our responsibilities, and to care for significant relationships. But inside we feel chaotic. Our internal furniture seems pulled to the center of our inner room with no apparent order, and our interior climate seems best described as unremitting grayness. This tension might reveal the paradox in our lives, that our inner and outer worlds contradict each other, and that weakness in the inner world can co-exist with power in the outer world.

In the early 1970's my outer life seemed to be working very well. I was Dean of the Jesuit School of Theology in Chicago, a successful teacher, an effective committee member, and productive in scholarly publication. People saw me as in charge of my world. Internally, as I later came to know, I was moving toward burnout, bumping into limits, living with unnamed inner conflicts, and moving with a pervasive sense of inadequacy. I felt inadequate most of the time, and I did not know why. My depression had no meaning, especially since my outer world continued to work well.

At this time I taught a course on the Gospel of John that I had taught several times before. I knew the material well, and I had learned how to teach it. I met with the class on Monday evenings for two and a half hours. As I prepared for each class, I felt inadequate and depressed.

I paced my office with my notes in hand and wanted to cancel the class. Fear gripped me, and anxiety all but paralyzed me. I wanted to run away rather than meet the students.

Somehow, however, I made it to the classroom each Monday night. Somehow I presented material and facilitated discussion. But I never felt anything but panic inside. In my judgment the course would succeed if the students did not demand their tuition refunded. At the last class, when they evaluated the course, most said that it was one of the best courses they had ever taken. I was stunned and startled. I could not explain the conflict between how I felt inside and what they experienced.

Experiences like this can teach us that when we feel weakest, we might be most powerful. Increased vulnerability often heightens our potential. We begin to find new meaning in the paradox that Paul preached. We resonate more deeply with his message that a crucified Christ reveals God's power and wisdom. For we have discovered this paradoxical truth in our lived experience. We begin to agree with him that when we are weak, we may be strong with a power other than our own. We hear his invitation to see our lives not as problems to be solved, but as mysteries to be lived. We let Paul draw us more deeply into that mystery of ourselves and the mystery of God's action in Jesus Christ.

In accepting paradox we no longer need to appear strong even when we feel weak, nor do we need to seem wise even when we feel foolish. For we gradually learn to have compassion on our weakness and within it to find new strength. We submit less to the temptation always to be self-sufficient. We let ourselves be weak when we are weak, strong when we are strong.

We also discover that our weakness can relate us profoundly to others. It allows us to share our common struggles with compassion and solidarity. Weakness denied isolates us from one another, but in admitting weakness we can mutually support each other. Finally, our weakness can relate us profoundly with God, since it is the place in which God's power is revealed. In the apparent weakness of a crucified Messiah, God revealed a paradoxical power and wisdom. God continues to reveal it in and through our human weakness. Aware of this paradox, we can hear God say to us, "My power is made perfect in weakness," and with Paul we can come to recognize that when we are weak, then are we strong.

Death and Resurrection

> I am reminding you, brothers, of the Gospel I preached
> to you which you indeed received.... For I transmitted
> to you at the outset what I myself had received, that

> Christ died for our sins according to the Scriptures, and
> that he was buried, and that he was raised on the third
> day according to the Scriptures, and that he appeared
> to Cephas, then to the twelve.... It is thus that we preach
> and thus that you have believed (1 Cor 15:1, 3-5, 11).

> Do you not know that all of us who have been baptized
> into Christ Jesus were baptized into his death? We were
> buried therefore with him by baptism into death, so
> that as Christ was raised from the dead by the glory of
> the Father, we too might walk in newness of life. For if
> we have been united with him in a death like his, we
> shall certainly be united with him in a resurrection like
> this (Rom 6:3-5).

> I have been crucified with Christ; it is no longer I who
> live, but Christ who lives in me; and the life I now live
> in the flesh I live by faith in the Son of God, who loved
> me and gave himself for me (Gal 2:19-20).

After God's revelation to him on the road to Damascus, Paul recognizes Jesus Christ crucified and risen as the center of his relationship to God. He opens himself in faith to Jesus Christ as the power by which he began to live. He accepts his call to preach Christ to the Gentiles.

When Paul preaches Christ's death and resurrection, some Corinthians believe his message and are baptized. Paul later recalls for the Corinthians what he had preached to them and what they had come to believe (1 Cor 15:1-11). He uses a traditional formula which both he and the Corinthians had accepted, since he found it compatible with his preaching. It also demonstrates his solidarity with the wider Christian movement.

Paul makes four statements about Jesus Christ. First, Christ died for our sins according to the Scriptures. Paul does not indicate how he died nor the meaning of his death. He merely states that his death was somehow related to our sins, and that it happened in accord with the plan God revealed in the Hebrew Scriptures.

Second, Christ was buried. This statement underscores the fact that he died, since a buried man is certainly counted among the dead.

Third, Christ was raised on the third day according to the Scriptures. God acted in history in a unique way to transform Jesus of Nazareth, so that he lives in glory as Lord. Since this action transcends human experience, it must be expressed in metaphors like God "exalted him," "designated him Son in power," "made him sit at his right hand." Paul favors the traditional metaphor that God "raised him from the dead." What matters is that the Christ who died and was buried has been freed from the power of death and lives with God as Lord.

Finally, Christ appeared to Cephas (Peter) and then to the twelve. Paul does not say when or how he appeared. He seems content with the fact that Jesus revealed to his closest followers that he was risen. His appearance assured them that he had triumphed over death. Paul then adds others to whom the risen Lord appeared, including himself. We have seen how he based his claim of being an apostle on that appearance.

Paul also describes the dynamics involved in his preaching and the Corinthians' response. He preached to them, and they received his preaching. He transmitted to them what he had received, and they believed his message. Their faith involved hearing his message about Jesus Christ and heeding its call for a response. It meant that they committed themselves to what they heard and submitted to it in obedience. It meant that they let go of their previous understandings and reached out for the mystery in Christ's death and resurrection.

Above all, the Corinthians responded as total persons to Paul and to what he preached. They trusted Paul enough to take his message seriously and not to dismiss it as absurd. They let it begin to inform and influence how they made meaning in their lives. They also trusted the God about whom Paul spoke and the Jesus Christ who died and was raised from the dead. Their faith enabled them to begin to swim less and float more, to drive less and take more buses.

Faith also meant that the Corinthians opened themselves to receive God's love as a pure, undeserved gift. God revealed his love in the death and resurrection of Jesus Christ. Faith opened them to the mystery of that event and to its power as a new life principle. Through Paul's preaching, God offered them his love as a gift, and they let go of whatever might prevent them from accepting it. They grew confident that God had gifted them in Christ Jesus and courageous in trusting that gift.

The rite of baptism marked initiation into the Christian community. In Paul's day adults were baptized by immersion. Children were baptized along with their parents and the other adults in their household. Since the rite itself had power to accomplish what it symbolized, every baptized person received the gift of the Spirit.

Imagine a circular pool with stairs leading into it on two sides. Persons to be baptized approach the pool dressed in flowing garments. As they remove their garments, men shield the nudity of the men, and women do the same for the women. Now they begin the action that symbolizes their letting go of the world they have known, so as to enter a new world. The men and later the women descend into the water to dramatize that they are being buried with Christ in death. As they come up from under the water, they profess that the Jesus, who died and was buried, was also raised from the dead. Finally, as they climb out of the pool, they know that they too have received new life. Before being dried, assistants anoint them with abundant oil and clothe them in a new, white garment.

Pauline Christians knew from this experience that they were baptized into Christ's death. As they moved down the stairs into the water, they moved into union with the mystery of his death and resurrection. They were buried under the water, as the dead Christ was buried. They were raised up out of the water, as Jesus was raised from the dead. Through this ritual passage they began to grow into union with Christ, as a branch grows into union with the tree on which it has been grafted. Since they have been united with him in death, they will also be united with him in resurrection.

Death and resurrection constituted one, inseparable reality for Jesus Christ. So those who participate in his death through baptism will also participate in his resurrection. Through baptism they have begun to live by a power other than their own. They have become one body with their fellow Christians. At the parousia their participation in Christ's resurrection will be complete when they are united forever with the risen Lord.

Faith and baptism are the means through which persons participate in God's saving action in Christ. They are absorbed into Christ, incorporated into his body, and assimilated into his death and resurrection. Their union with Christ can be called mystical in the sense that they begin to experience him more as the inner power by which they live than as a person outside themselves with whom they enjoy deep communion. They live in Christ. His death and resurrection enables them to find meaning in their lives. For they are members of the one body of Christ, and they live as branches on the tree that is Christ.

Paul gives equal weight to the death and resurrection of Jesus Christ. It is one reality, one mystery, one revelation of God's power, one manifestation of Christ's love. So the cross at center stage is much more than the instrument by which Christ died. It has been transformed from a means of execution into a positive symbol of death and life. It is the form through which Paul experienced the power of God's love.

Paul has passed through a death that has enabled him to live with a new perspective on everything—on himself, others, the law, and God. Baptism enacted his dying and rising, and Paul continues to live out his baptism in everyday life. Since he has died with Christ, he does not consider his life his own. He is still Paul. But he now lives by a power centered no longer in himself but in Jesus Christ. He was given that power when he experienced the risen Lord. Faith enables him to continue to live by the power that is Jesus Christ and the Holy Spirit.

Paul preached that Christ died and was raised from the dead, and Jews and Gentiles trusted both the man and his message enough to be baptized. We are invited to do the same especially in our celebration of Lent and Eastertide. We ask that our faith be deepened. Paul opened himself in faith to Jesus Christ as the power by which he began to live. He invited the Corinthians to the same surrender. Now he invites us to swim less and float more, to drive less and take more buses.

When we trust, we accept Paul and his message. We allow him to shape us, as individuals and communities. We also trust his message about Jesus Christ crucified and risen. We rely on it, begin to act on it, and let it shape our view of reality. Because that message touches the roots of our human existence, it asks for a deep and strong commitment. For we are shaped by whom and what we can trust, by what we can count on in life. Our networks of trusts constitute our identity as persons. Paul invites us to ground our trusts in the God who revealed his love in the death and resurrection of Jesus Christ.

Paul and the Corinthians also opened themselves to receive God's love as a pure gift. They challenge us to do the same. Responding is not easy in a culture that says we must earn whatever we get and not expect to always get what we deserve. Paul counters with the basic stance that God has given us life and all else as a simple gift. How are we at receiving gifts from one another? Do we dismiss them without receiving them? Are we so caught up with responding that we fail to hear what the other person has said? Paul invites us to grow into the attitude that God has given us life as an undeserved gift, and that God revealed the gift of his love in Christ's death and resurrection. He urges us actively to receive God's gift in faith and to live by that faith even when it conflicts with the culture around us.

By their baptism the Corinthians were united with Jesus Christ. They began to participate in the mystery of his death and resurrection. Many of us, who were baptized as infants, did not know what that action meant. As adults, however, we are invited to renew our baptism and discover its deeper meaning in our lives. If we believe that through baptism we have been united to Christ's death and begin to participate in his resurrection, then we can reflect on that union for the meaning it might reveal in apparently meaningless suffering. Suffering may begin to make sense as our sharing in the death of Christ and our participation in the power of his resurrection.

Equality, Community, and Eucharist

> For as many of you as were baptized into Christ have put on Christ. There is neither Jew nor Greek, there is neither slave nor free, there is neither male nor female; for you are all one in Christ Jesus (Gal 3:27-28).

> Now there are varieties of gifts, but the same Spirit; and there are varieties of service, but the same Lord; and there are varieties of working, but it is the same God who inspires them all in every one.... For just as the body is one and has many members, and all the members of the body, though many, are one body, so it is with Christ. For by one Spirit we were all baptized into one body—Jews or Greeks, slaves or free—and all were made to drink of one Spirit.... If one member suffers, all suffer together; if one member is honored, all rejoice together. Now you are the body of Christ and individually members of it (1 Cor 12:4-6, 12-13, 26-27).

> The cup of blessing which we bless, is it not a participation in the blood of Christ? The bread which we break, is it not a participation in the body of Christ? Because there is one bread, we who are many are one body, for we all partake of the one bread (1 Cor 10:16-17).

Baptism initiated the early Christians into a community in which they were to live out their incorporation into Christ. As they rose from the water to be anointed and clothed in a white garment, they began to realize that they were putting on Christ, not as an outer garment but as the inner power by which they began to live. From that moment they were to live in communities characterized by radical equality among its members, mutual cooperation and support, and the Eucharist.

Aware that they were one in Christ, Christians began to resist the social tensions in their culture, namely, the racism, classism, and sexism of the Hellenistic world (Gal 3:27-28). As we have seen, tension between Jews and Greeks raised important questions for the first Christians. Paul devoted his missionary zeal and powers of persuasion to demonstrate that in Christ there is neither Jew nor Greek. The success of his mission to the Gentiles must be explained as God's plan for the salvation of the world. It would take several decades, however, before Paul's view that Jews and Gentiles were equal in Christ would be widely accepted.

A similar tension existed between slaves and their masters. The first century Mediterranean world was built on the distinction between slavery and privilege. A person's status mostly depended on birth, but also on wealth. Although moving to a higher level of income and a more affluent life-style was difficult, some born as slaves did make their way into the aristocracy. Within the Christian community, however, masters and slaves were expected to pray together as equals and to sit down at the same table. For they knew that they were brothers and sisters in the same Lord.

Sexist tension between male and female existed in Paul's world. Women were subordinate to men. Paul counters that cultural attitude with the reminder that as they came from the creating hand of God, male and female were equal and not subordinate. Life in the Christian community was to mirror that divine order and celebrate the equality of men and women without denying their sexual differences. Both had access to salvation in Jesus Christ. Neither male nor female had any advantage or disadvantage in the community. Members had to recognize and resist destructive tensions based on racism, classism, and sexism. For all had been baptized into the same Lord and had drunk of the same Spirit.

Baptism also created the community as the body of Christ (1 Cor 12:1-31; Rom 12:3-8). In the Hellenistic society of Paul's time, the metaphor of the body was applied to the state as the body politic. Paul meant it to express more than a union of citizens conspiring for the common good of peace and well-being. He saw resemblances between a Christian community and a physical body. Its flesh and bones, its circulatory, glandular, and nervous systems, its entire self all work together for the good of the whole body. So all individual Christians, whatever their race, class or sex, were to work together to build community as the body of Christ. All were baptized into Jesus Christ crucified and risen and made to drink of the one Spirit. That Spirit enabled them to set aside the roles that separate Jew from Greek, slave from free, male from female in the Hellenistic world. In community they lived with each other as equals in Christ.

With this understanding Paul addressed the tensions reported to him from Corinth. Differing gifts had led the members to compete with each other. Some gifts appeared more extraordinary than others, and their beneficiaries began to assume an air of superiority. Less fortunate members felt dissatisfied with their gifts, while others wondered whether they had received any gifts at all.

Paul responded by naming resemblances between the community and a human body and by identifying the community as the body of

Christ. Each member can make a unique contribution to the human body. So God assigned different gifts to each one in the community. The community is to celebrate each one's gifts as contributing to its overall life and growth. Diversity must be maintained among the members, but it must be balanced by their underlying unity in Christ. As an exaggerated diversity will destroy the community, so an overemphasis on unity will stifle its spontaneity and creativity. The Corinthians must work to maintain a creative balance between their different gifts and their oneness in the same Spirit and Lord.

In a human body the different parts also interact and depend on each other. The hand needs the foot, and the eye needs the ear. What seem the less important, more private parts of the body prove to be the most indispensable and are treated with most respect. Similarly, as community members celebrate their differences, they are also to recognize how much they depend upon each other. Interdependence means that when one member suffers, the others enter into that person's pain with compassion and solidarity. When one member rejoices, the others join in his or her celebration. For baptism into the same Christ empowers them to live together with more compassion than dissension, with more cooperation than competition.

At the Eucharist the Corinthians remembered that Christ died and was raised from the dead, celebrated his presence among them, and looked forward with confidence to his coming in glory. In warning them not to worship idols, Paul takes for granted that they recognize Christ in the cup that they drink and in the bread that they eat (1 Cor 10:16-17). The bond established in baptism deepens in the Eucharist. For by sharing in the body and blood of Christ they are united both to him and to each other. Eating the one bread and drinking from the same cup continually builds them into a community that makes Christ present in the world.

When the Corinthians gathered for the meal prior to the Eucharist, some members ate better than others. When Paul heard about this abuse, he pointed out how their actions were inconsistent with the Eucharist they were about to celebrate. They profaned the body and blood of the Lord (1 Cor 11:17-34). If at the first meal they were not one, how could they express their unity in the Eucharist by partaking of the same bread and drinking of the same cup?

Paul also reminded them that "as often as you eat this bread and drink the cup, you proclaim the Lord's death until he comes" (1 Cor 11:26). For the Eucharist enacts in ritual that Christ died for our sins, that he was raised from the dead on the third day, and that he will come again in glory to complete his work.

Our life in community today also carries tensions between races, economic classes, and the sexes. We also struggle to keep our balance between unity and diversity. In a multi-racial parish, for example, parishioners may disagree about how they can maintain their identity, while meeting the liturgical needs of Hispanic, Oriental, black, and Anglo-Saxon members. Similarly, men and women bring different gifts to their religious communities. Diversity may at times seem to threaten unity, and unity may at other times seem to stifle very rich but differing gifts. Finally, women desire to be equal to men in Church and society, so that they might develop what they have been given and realize their potential as members of the body of Christ.

Paul does not provide neat solutions to these unavoidable, complex tensions. He does, however, provide a perspective from which to address them. He urges that we not forget that we have all been baptized into the same Lord and drink of the same Spirit. He challenges us, as individuals and faith communities, to let go of the guises that normally separate us into racial groups, economic brackets, and sexual stereotypes, so that we might live as equal in Christ. He reminds us that, like a human body, we cannot exist together without cherishing our diversity and using our gifts to build the communities to which we belong. He asks us never to forget how much we need and depend on each other, as different parts of the same body of Christ.

Transitions in our adult lives can be either traumatic or developmental. A traumatic transition happens when an external event—an unexpected illness, the death of a loved one, a crippling accident, a divorce or separation, a son or daughter opposing family values—shatters our way of making meaning and leaves us suspended in midair. A developmental transition is caused by the normal, predictable patterns in adult life—young adulthood, midlife, retirement, aging. In all adult transitions the meaning we have known begins to collapse, and we feel afraid and embarrassed, anxious and depressed. Negotiating such transitions successfully involves recruiting persons to support us with patience and compassion and to challenge us with care and honesty.

What support groups or communities have you experienced or do you know about? How do the members help each other find meaning in their suffering? Twelve-step groups help members recover from addiction to such things as alcohol, drugs, sex, overeating, and gambling. Other groups are formed around traumas such as separation, divorce, or suicide. Still others focus on normal adult transitions such as midlife, retirement, and aging. In charismatic and cursillo groups people find support in prayer. Doctors and lawyers, priests and ministers, and other professional persons gather to reflect on the deep transitions that are taking place in their professions.

Support communities are characterized by solidarity and compassion. Solidarity means that we move into the depths of our own lives to discover that we are all brothers and sisters. We come to know that another's pain is not separate from our own and that a deep bond connects every human life with every other human life. Compassion means that we go where others are hurting, enter into their places of pain, and share in their brokenness and fear, in their confusion and anguish. Both solidarity and compassion enable us to be weak with the weak, vulnerable with the vulnerable, and powerless with the powerless. Both invite us to share with others our common human condition. Paul described the same reality: "If one member suffers, all suffer together; if one member is honored, all rejoice together" (1 Cor 12:26).

In the Eucharist we too recall Christ's death, celebrate his presence as risen Lord, and look forward to his coming in glory. We say "Christ *has* died. Christ *is* risen. Christ *will* come again." In eating the same bread and drinking from the same cup we remind ourselves that we have all been baptized into the same body of Christ. In Corinth the community members, about seventy-five in all, must have known each other well. They could easily have experienced the bond between them at the Eucharist. Realizing that we are one body in Christ is more difficult when we participate in a large parish Eucharist with people whom we may never know. Smaller, basic Christian communities within a parish might provide a better setting for finding the meaning in Paul's statements about our unity and equality in Christ.

Dynamics of Suffering

We have this treasure in earthen vessels, to show that the transcendent power belongs to God and not to us. We are afflicted in every way, but not crushed; perplexed, but not driven to despair; persecuted, but not forsaken; struck down, but not destroyed; always carrying in the body the death of Jesus so that the life of Jesus may also be manifested in our bodies (2 Cor 4:7-10).

More than that, we rejoice in our sufferings, knowing that suffering produces endurance, and endurance produces character, and character produces hope, and hope does not disappoint us, because God's love has been poured into our hearts through the Holy Spirit which has been given to us (Rom 5:3-5).

I am sure that neither death, nor life, nor angels, nor
principalities, nor things present, nor things to come,
nor powers, nor height, nor depth, nor anything else in
all creation, will be able to separate us from the love of
God in Christ Jesus our Lord (Rom 8:38-39).

Paul's convictions about power in weakness and about his union
with Christ's death and resurrection enabled him to find meaning in
his suffering. Paul was not a stranger to suffering. When Christian
missionaries visited the churches that he had founded in Galatia, they
preached a gospel different from the one he had preached. They accused
Paul of watering down the requirements for Gentile membership in the
community. They even challenged his claim to be an apostle of Jesus
Christ. Paul responded with the angry letter we know as Galatians.

Missionaries, whom Paul later called "superlative apostles," attacked
his credentials and his message at Corinth. Relations between Paul and
his beloved community deteriorated to the point of crisis and confrontation.
After a letter written "with many tears" the Corinthians and Paul began
to be reconciled.

In what may be that letter written with tears Paul boasts about his
labors and imprisonments, about the forty lashes and countless beatings
he endured, about his shipwreck and arduous journeys, about dangers
from his own people, from false brethren, and from Gentiles, about his
hunger, thirst, and sleepless nights, and about his constant anxiety for
his communities.

How did Paul find meaning in such apparently meaningless suffering?
In Second Corinthians he compares himself to an "earthen vessel," that
is, to a small clay pot that was used in homes as a water container or
an oil lamp. It was weak and fragile, easily broken and quickly replaced.
Paul knew himself to be weak and fragile, so that others might recognize
that the power in his ministry was from God. Suffering had continued
to reveal the paradox of God at work in his apparent brokenness.

Paul then describes the pattern of sufferings which, though real,
did not overwhelm him. He was afflicted in every way. Affliction often
crushes the person afflicted. But Paul was not crushed. He was perplexed,
and perplexity can drive a person to despair. But he was not driven to
despair. Paul was persecuted, and in persecution a person can easily
feel forsaken. But Paul did not feel forsaken. He was struck down with
a blow that might have destroyed him. But Paul was not destroyed. Paul
knew real suffering, but it did not overpower him, nor did it destroy his
human spirit. For God's power kept him from being crushed, driven to
despair, forsaken, and destroyed.

Paul then recognizes in his suffering the pattern of Christ's death and resurrection. His being afflicted, perplexed, persecuted, struck down meant that he carried in his body the death of Jesus. His not being crushed, driven to despair, forsaken, and destroyed meant that the life of Jesus was also manifested in his body. Paul had preached that God's power was revealed in the weakness of a crucified messiah, and that Christ died and was raised from the dead. He opened himself in faith to receive the gift of God's love, and he invited others to participate in Christ's death and resurrection through faith and baptism. His faith now enabled him to find meaning in his suffering. For he recognized in it his sharing in the death of Christ and his knowing the power of Christ's resurrection: "While we live, we are always being given up to death for Jesus' sake, so that the life of Jesus may be manifested in our mortal flesh" (2 Cor 4:11).

In Romans, Paul rejoices in his sufferings, since they can produce endurance, strengthen character, and lead to hope (Rom 5:3-5). At first Paul may sound like a masochist, since he seems to take delight in pain for its own sake. But he does not say that he wanted suffering, sought it, or even liked it. Yet experience taught him that suffering is unavoidable in human life. So he describes the dynamics by which pain can lead to new possibilities. It can call forth untapped powers for endurance. Over time, endurance can strengthen character. Strong character can enable the suffering person to hope, that is, to choose life even in a death-like situation. Finally, hope will not disappoint the believer. For it is grounded in the love of God that was revealed in Christ crucified and risen, and that was poured into our hearts by the Holy Spirit.

Hope means having the freedom and the power to choose life even in death-like situations. Despair is the opposite decision to let death exercise its power. Hope happens in the choice of life over death. It is experienced as a life-giving power that lifts persons out of the clutches of pain and enables them to see in the pain the seeds of new possibilities. Hope may or may not be accompanied with hopeful feelings or sensible consolation. But it empowers believers to wait for new life to happen through suffering, and it enables them to trust a power greater than suffering or death.

Paul knew the meaning of hope from his own suffering. He was confident that others would find the same process at work in their sufferings. For Paul was convinced that no created power, not even suffering or death, could separate Christians from the power of God's love in Christ Jesus our Lord (Rom 8:38-39).

Paul found meaning in apparently meaningless suffering by recognizing in it his participation in the dying and rising of Christ. Can we do the same? Mrs. Mary Walters, a fifty-three year old black woman and mother of six children, has lived her entire life in the Chicago ghettos. Her husband, a severe alcoholic, practically drank himself to death. One son almost destroyed himself with drugs and alcohol. Brain-damaged and burnt out, he now haunts the neighborhood. He depends on his mother to rescue him from critical situations. Some years ago Mary herself was diagnosed to be suffering from inoperable brain cancer. With a poor prognosis and after painful therapy, she surprised her doctors with an amazing recovery.

Mary still lives in one of the poorest neighborhoods on Chicago's south side. An active neighborhood leader, she is often called upon to represent her black community at political and religious meetings. In what seemed an impossible situation she has been able not merely to survive but to find a meaningful life. A deep faith sustains her in each crisis, as she attributes her strength not to herself but to God's power in her life. Others see her as a sign of trust and hope in a neighborhood where fear and hopelessness prevail. She sees her life as a gift and a call to minister to others. Her suffering and her life situation have not overwhelmed or dehumanized her. Nor has she lost her power or freedom to fight back. Her human spirit empowered by God has enabled her to hope against hope. She chooses life in her death-like situation, and she calls others to join her in their common struggle against forces that threaten to destroy their lives.

Paul found meaning in his apparently meaningless suffering by identifying in it a dynamic process that moved from suffering to endurance, from endurance to character, and from character to hope. Can we discover that same process in our suffering? Martha and Dick were married for several years before they had their first child. When they became pregnant, they were delighted and began to look forward with joy to the birth of that first child. In the birthing Martha was given too much medication. Elizabeth was born severely retarded. She would have been normal, had it not been for the overdose of medicine.

For fourteen years Martha and Dick have cared for Beth with extraordinary patience and love. For the first few years they kept her in their home and provided the constant care that her situation demanded. But as Beth grew older and as two healthy boys were added to the family, Martha and Dick made the difficult decision to place Beth in a home for the severely retarded. Her parents and brothers visit her regularly, even though she shows little awareness of their presence. Beth will die before too many years, and her death will be both a deep sorrow and a relief.

Martha and Dick have learned much from their daughter about the meaning of life. She has enabled them to discover how suffering has

called forth endurance, how their endurance has given them strong
character, and how their strong character empowers them with hope.
They have been able to choose life and remain in that choice even in
their heartrending situation.

Vision of the Future

> But we would not have you ignorant, brethren, concerning
> those who are asleep, that you may not grieve as others
> do who have no hope. For since we believe that Jesus
> died and rose again, even so, through Jesus, God will
> bring with him those who have fallen asleep.... For the
> Lord himself will descend from heaven with a cry of
> command, with the archangel's call, and with the sound
> of the trumpet of God. And the dead in Christ will rise
> first; then we who are alive, who are left, shall be caught
> up together with them in the clouds to meet the Lord
> in the air; and so we shall always be with the Lord.
> Therefore, comfort one another with these words (1
> Thes 4:13-14, 16-18).

> Then comes the end, when he (Christ) delivers the
> kingdom to God the Father after destroying every rule
> and every authority and power. For he must reign until
> he has put all enemies under his feet. The last enemy
> to be destroyed is death.... When all things are subjected
> to him, then the Son himself will also be subjected to
> him who put all things under him, that God may be
> everything to every one (1 Cor 15:24-26, 28).

Paul next describes a vision of the future that enables Christians
to find meaning in their suffering. He writes to answer the concern of
the community at Thessalonica. Some of their members had died. In
mourning them the others wondered whether the deceased would participate with them in the second coming of the Lord. Paul comforted
them with the assurance that those still living at the Lord's coming will
not have any advantage over those who have died.

Christian grief differs from pagan sadness in that it is not without
hope. It is characterized by the realization that death is not the end and
that life lies beyond death. The Thessalonians could have hope and be
joyful even as they mourned the loss of their loved ones. For they believed
that Jesus died and was raised from the dead. In their baptism they
began to participate in his death and resurrection. They later recognized

sufferings as their further share in that mystery. Now as they mourn the dead with hope, they are to know that, when the Lord comes, both they and the deceased will be united with him forever.

Paul next describes how Jesus will come. He focuses on those elements which accompany the Lord's descent from heaven. The cry of command, the archangel's call, and the sound of a trumpet that accompany the Lord's descent will signal that the old age has ended and that the fullness of the new age has dawned. Paul then tells how those who have died will rise and move upward with the living to join the Lord in the air. At that moment the union begun in baptism and continued in their lives, as individuals and communities, will be made perfect. For they shall always be with the Lord.

Paul completes this picture of the end time when he writes to the Corinthians about the resurrection from the dead. The Lord will reign until all enemies have been brought under submission. Death will be the last enemy to submit to him. But it too will recognize that in Christ God has overthrown its power. When all things are subject to the Lord, then the Lord himself will be subjected to God. God will be all in all. This vision of the future with its ultimate optimism grounds Paul's conviction that nothing, not even suffering or death, can separate Christians from the love of God in Christ Jesus the Lord.

How we think about and imagine the future strongly influences how we find meaning in meaningless suffering. Thoughts and images of the future swim around inside us whether explicitly or implicitly, consciously or unconsciously. Sometimes we are drawn toward the future, sometimes we dread it. We may look forward to it as fulfilling our deepest dreams and desires. Or we live in mortal fear of eternal damnation. In any case, our images and thoughts about the future influence how we live in the present.

Many think that death marks the end of everything. Life does not exist after death. Since suffering is an ally of death, it is an enemy to be resisted at all cost. It must be erased as a human evil. It diminishes the only life we will ever have. We cannot hope to find any meaning in it. Other people believe that death is not the end, but that we will return to this world to begin a new life. In that reincarnation the quality of our life will depend on how we live now. We are to accept our lives with their pleasure and pain, their joys and sufferings. For pain and suffering belong to the long process of purification that will continue through many reincarnations. If we live well with present suffering and pain, we will return to a higher life in the next reincarnation.

Paul sees individuals and communities who believe in Christ as destined to live beyond death. Death is not the end, nor will Christians be reincarnated. They will be united to the Lord, and with him they shall be one with God. Paul's vision can enable us to confront meaningless pain and suffering, even death itself, and say to them, "You are not the end." For we believe that, as Christ died and was raised, so we must suffer, die and be raised. Pain may seem like the end, but it can lead to new possibilities. Suffering may seem like the end, but it can lead to hope in the Spirit. Death may seem like the end of everything, but it leads to eternal life.

We may not find much meaning in Paul's scene of the Lord descending from heaven with the sound of a trumpet and the archangel's call. We may find it hard to imagine the dead rising up to join the living and moving upward with them to meet the Lord in the air. Paul's scenario may seem distant and strange, but his message challenges us to think about the future and to create our own script. For how we think about and imagine the future informs how we search for meaning in meaningless suffering.

We have studied Paul's message about dying and rising in Christ. We have reflected on how it might help us find meaning in meaningless suffering. Paul has preached about God revealing his paradoxical power and wisdom in Jesus Christ crucified and risen from the dead. He has invited us to open ourselves in faith to receive that revelation and participate in it through baptism. We have suggested how this paradox might resonate with our increased vulnerability in times of transition. It might enable us to be compassionate with our weakness and expect to find within it new strength.

Paul has told us that whatever separates Jew from Greek, slave from free, male from female dissolves into a radical oneness based on baptism into the same Lord. Faith communities are the body of Christ. In the Eucharist their unity is expressed as they proclaim his death until he comes. They eat one bread and drink from one cup to symbolize their unity. We have reflected on how we must struggle to maintain a creative balance between unity and diversity in our faith communities. Support, compassion and solidarity are essential to the process of finding meaning in our adult lives.

Paul saw the pattern of Christ's dying and rising in his own suffering. We recognized how suffering can lead to hope in the Spirit. That hope enabled him to look toward a future when the risen Lord would complete the union begun in baptism. We have described contemporary persons in whom the same dynamics are at work, as they respond to their pain. We have seen how our view of the future contributes to how we make meaning of meaningless suffering.

Now I want to return to the cases described at the beginning of this chapter. Ed chose to die. He did not want to undergo a second kidney transplant or live with a dialysis machine. He chose his own death so that his wife Helen and their children might have a better life. He chose to be buried with Christ in death so that they might walk in newness of life. Ed saw his death as participating in Christ's death. As Christ rose from the dead, he hoped that his family might enjoy a better life, and that he might live with the risen Lord.

Edward's hopes for his family were realized. At first Helen and the children experienced his death as the end of everything. For a long time they endured an almost desperate grief for their father and husband. But gradually their mourning turned into an inner strength. They began to see new possibilities in their lives. Ed's love sustained them as they moved through suffering that seemed totally meaningless. It strengthened them to create a new life together. Helen has since married a man who loved and respected Ed. She has given birth to two children. She will never stop missing Ed. But the love that Ed expressed in choosing death has enabled Helen and their children to see apparently meaningless suffering in the light of Christ's death and resurrection.

At first Bill and Randy were bitter about the inflation that had killed their dreams for retirement. They remained angry, sad, and even depressed for many months. Life seemed cruel and unfair. One day, however, they asked themselves how long they wanted to live bitter, angry, and sad lives. After all, they continued to enjoy good health. Above all they still had each other. Weren't health and companionship more important than travel and sightseeing? Could they respond to the meaningless suffering in their situation instead of letting it overwhelm them? Slowly Bill and Randy began to accept their limited situation.

With acceptance they could begin to imagine new possibilities, different activities, wider interests. They began to explore what was possible within their fixed income. Dark clouds gradually lifted as they began to sense a happiness that would not have been theirs without the painful disappointment. Pain had not deprived them of all power to respond. First they responded with anger and bitterness, but gradually they found the freedom and imagination to create a meaningful life together. They had not chosen the pain, sought it, or liked it. But they did endure it without knowing why it happened. Endurance enabled them to touch an inner strength, and hope lifted them up to see new possibilities for their remaining years.

As adults, we all expect to experience patterns of dying and rising, of suffering without apparent meaning. At times we find life emptying out rather than filling up, and we experience the world-out-of-joint where best-laid plans go awry. Thus we experience mortality, the human condition that will terminate in death. We suffer throughout life because we are permanently taking leave, permanently parting with dreams and persons, permanently looking toward the end, permanently looking for God. Suffering and death are present in adult life as the absurd and meaningless, as the inevitable waste in lives that never fulfill their promise, as the evils that will not be fitted into any reasonable plan. We all suffer at times without knowing why.

Paul sets forth the drama of God's action in Jesus Christ, a drama of universal significance, in which we participate as individuals and communities. His message can give meaning and purpose to our lives with their fluctuating patterns of pleasure and pain, strength and weakness, hope and despair, life and death. Paul's message can make pain and loss, our own or that of others, and even death itself not only tolerable but meaningful. Suffering and death are not the enemy. Empty, meaningless suffering and death are our adversary. But for Paul our suffering and death are significant, because in them we participate in the suffering and death of Jesus Christ. As God raised Jesus from the dead, so he will raise us from death to life with the risen Lord. Suffering and death may still be heartrending, but they are not without meaning.

Perhaps you would like to reflect on this chapter by responding to the following questions:

■ What do you think of how Paul found meaning in his life? What attracts you? What do you find difficult?
■ What words do you think of when you search for meaning? What do you do? Where do you go?
■ Does Paul's search for meaning help you in your search? If so, how? If not, why not?
■ What strength, what message, does your baptism into Christ's death and resurrection give you?
■ What communities provide support when your life seems empty and without meaning?
■ When have you experienced the paradox of power working in your apparent weakness?
■ What is your vision of the future? How does it enable you to find meaning in your present life?

6

God's Plan of Action for the World

Conflicts at times shatter our world of meaning, conflicts between our deepest, most cherished convictions and the facts of our concrete, lived experience. For example, we are convinced that all Americans are meant to participate in the economy, but we grow tense as facts force us to recognize the widening gap between rich and poor, between those who participate and those who are disenfranchised. We are convinced that the United States and the Soviet Union are meant to inhabit the earth in harmony and peace, but endless talk and more sophisticated weapons make us fear a nuclear holocaust.

We are also convinced that stable marriages and strong families assure a healthy society, but the high divorce rate, the stress in parent-child relations, the multiplication of single-parent families, the consequences for the next generation of children challenge those convictions and make us wonder what family life will be like in the future.

We are convinced that, as human persons, we were created to live together in justice and harmony, in love and peace, but the television news reminds us each night that violent crimes are increasing, that the drug culture is expanding, and that terrorism continues to threaten international security. We are convinced that God is present and active in all these events, but at times we must ask whether God has gone on leave or fallen asleep.

Conflicts between our convictions and our experience create an inner tension that can send us on a search for meaning. What can we do? Are we powerless? Can we come together to change our world? Are there stories to explain the conflicts, values that we might recover, and images of power that say we can still live in hope? Where is God? Does God have a plan for our world? How can we know the divine order? How can we continue to believe in God's presence and action in the world?

Paul wrestled with similar conflicts between his deepest convictions about God and the facts of his mission to the Gentiles. He was firmly convinced that God had chosen the Jews, but that through Jesus Christ he had also offered salvation to the Gentiles. When Jesus died on the cross and was raised from the dead, both Jews and Greeks had equal access to salvation through faith and baptism. Paul was also convinced that the same God had called him to preach Jesus Christ to the Gentiles.

Gentiles responded to Paul's preaching, but most Jews rejected his message. Paul experienced conflict between his convictions and his missionary experience. That conflict created a deep inner tension: "I am speaking the truth in Christ, I am not lying; my conscience bears me witness in the Holy Spirit, that I have great sorrow and unceasing anguish in my heart. For I could wish that I myself were accursed and cut off from Christ for the sake of my brethren, my kinsmen by race" (Rom 9:1-3). Had God's plan failed in its most crucial moment? Was there meaning in the conflict between Paul's confidence in God's fidelity and Israel's refusal to accept Jesus Christ? Paul's dilemma led him to recall the story of God's plan for the world and to retell it in a way that would enable him to make meaning of his experience.

Stories help us find meaning, if they tell of actions and events that are particularly important and significant for individuals and the world, especially for the world of persons. Such stories originate in the shared life of a community, bear the marks of its culture, and persist over generations as part of its tradition. They often articulate the origins of the community (Gen 1-2) or the main events that have shaped its life (exodus, death-resurrection of Jesus). Often they confront the polarities that a community experiences in its living together (humiliation and exaltation, poverty and wealth, despair and hope, death and life, falsehood and truth). Opposites can cohere with each other, as the stories are told and retold. For stories succeed in balancing contradictions that thought cannot hold in tension.

Stories also bring together disparate elements in life and articulate an entire world. They create a large and flexible landscape that can provide direction into the future, enable us to choose what is valuable in the present, and make us at home with our past. Without stories we do not know where we are, where we came from, where we are going, what is of value. Communities prize stories that suggest or are believed to explain what is most important in life. With such power, stories become inseparable and indispensable. Members retell, enact, and celebrate their stories in rituals of word, song, and action.

As a way to find meaning in the conflict between his faith convictions and his concrete experience, Paul recalls and retells the story of God's plan of action for the world. He recalls stories from his Jewish tradition, incorporates elements from the Hellenistic culture, and, above all, adds what he has learned in his conversion experience and his mission to the Gentiles. He doesn't tell the whole story in any one place. The different parts are scattered throughout his letters. But as he reflects on God's plan, Paul comes to know where he came from, where he is now, and where he is going. The story shows him how his present conflict fits into the larger landscape, that is, into God's plan for the salvation of Jews and Gentiles. With that meaning he can continue his mission to the Gentiles.

Paul's story resembles those told in the apocalyptic movement in Judaism. God had revealed secrets about the imminent end of the world and had given certain seers a message for the chosen people. People in the apocalyptic movement were children of both despair and hope—despair about the present course of human history and hope in the invincible power of God in the world.

Basic to Jewish faith was the conviction that God had created the world and continued to rule over creation. But the Jews knew that they had experienced more difficult than prosperous times in the world that their God had created. Babylonians had conquered them and led them into exile. The Jews returned to their homeland, but only when their Persian rulers approved. Independence under the Maccabeans was followed by Roman conquest, by the hated rule of Herod the Great, and by direct Roman control over Jerusalem and the temple. For Jews at home and in the diaspora this intolerable situation conflicted with their cherished beliefs about God's fidelity to them and God's reign over the world.

Was human history rushing to a foreordained tragic end? Had God abandoned them in the present time to the evil powers of Roman domination? That seemed to be what their experience told them. But basic to their faith was the belief that the present horrors were part of some hidden plan according to which God will intervene to end the present age and introduce a new age. Evil would then be destroyed and God's people would be forever blessed.

Paul preached that the new age had already begun with the death and resurrection of Jesus Christ, and that it will be completely established at his triumphant return. Between these two events, those who believe, both Jews and Gentiles, participate in the new age but are not altogether free from the old age. Christians are *already* saved from the old age but *not yet* fully saved. So they are to live as though already saved, but also with their eyes fixed on the future, that is, on their resurrection from the dead and their final union with the Lord.

Paul recalled past events and reinterpreted them from this apocalyptic perspective. Christians, whether Jews or Gentiles, are to live creatively within the tension between the two ages. Futhermore, Paul divides salvation history into three periods: from Adam to Moses, from Moses to Christ, from Christ to the parousia. We will now focus on key elements in his story: Adam and Christ, the Jewish law, Abraham—faith in the promise, and salvation for Gentiles and Jews.

Recall the scene with the cross at center stage. Behind it and a bit above are the men and women who act in God's plan for the world. We recognize persons from the past, like Adam and Abraham. We gradually identify Jews and Gentiles, persons like sin and death, and the law. As they move about, they reenact Paul's story of how God acted in the world. It is a cosmic, historical drama which situates the cross in the broader landscape of salvation history. As the story unfolds, we will reflect on how it enabled Paul to find meaning in the conflict between his convictions and his experience and on what it might contribute to our making meaning in similar situations.

Adam and Christ

> For as by a man came death, by a man has come also the resurrection of the dead. For as in Adam all die, so also in Christ shall all be made alive (1 Cor 15:21-22).

> Therefore, as sin came into the world through one man and death through sin, and so death spread to all men because all men had sinned. Sin indeed was in the world before the law was given, but sin is not counted where there is no law.... For if many died through one man's trespass, much more the grace of God and the free gift in the grace of that one man Jesus Christ abounded for many.... If, because of one man's trespass, death reigned through that one man, much more will those who receive the abundance of grace and the free gift of righteousness reign in life through the one man Jesus Christ. Then as one man's trespass led to condemnation for all men, so one man's act of righteousness leads to acquittal and life for all men. For as by one man's disobedience many were made sinners, so by one man's obedience many will be made righteous (Rom 5:12-21).

With Adam, sin and death took the stage as leading actors in the drama of salvation history. We normally think of sin as a specific action like murder or stealing, a particular transgression of a law or regulation.

But Paul sees sin as a force or power at work in the world. He personifies it to show how it acted to lead people to death. Adam's transgression brought sin into the cosmic drama. Sin brought with it death. Biological death was a sign of spiritual death. Adam, "the type of the one to come," started the tide of evil in the world. Sin was the power behind a flood of transgressions. Death was the end result. As inseparable allies, sin and death ravaged the created world to introduce inhuman conditions that would remain long after Adam and be reinforced by subsequent transgressions.

When Jesus Christ, "the one who was to come," died on the cross and was raised from the dead, he conquered sin and death. He reversed the tide of evil with a flow of forgiveness and life. Adam introduced sin as the power leading to death, but Christ introduced grace as the counterforce that leads to life. Adam's disobedience brought judgment and condemnation, but Christ's obedience carried acquittal and justification.

Contrasts between Adam and Christ, between type and anti-type, imply that the sinful status of all persons can be traced to Adam. Sin and death had power over Gentiles and Jews alike: "All have sinned and fall short of the glory of God" (Rom 3:23). Paul indicts the Gentiles for their ungodliness and wickedness (Rom 1:18-32). For they could have honored and thanked God from what they knew of God in creation. But sin kept them in bondage to lesser beings and elemental spirits (Gal 4:8-9).

Paul also indicted his fellow Jews. They took pride in the Mosaic law, as a sign of God's privilege and a sure guide to salvation. Jews may have possessed the law, but they did not observe it. Neither their circumcisions nor their observances could protect them from the all-pervasive power of sin. So before Christ, Jews and Gentiles alike were estranged from God and in bondage to the powers of sin and death.

The Jewish Law

> Now before faith came, we were confined under the law, kept under restraint until faith should be revealed. So the law was our custodian until Christ came, that we might be justified by faith. But now that faith has come, we are no longer under a custodian; for in Christ Jesus you are all sons of God, through faith (Gal 3:23-26).

> Likewise, my brethren, you have died to the law through the body of Christ, so that you may belong to another, to him who has been raised from the dead in order that we may bear fruit for God. While we were living in the

flesh, our sinful passions, aroused by the law, were at work in our members to bear fruit for death. But now we are discharged from the law, dead to that which held us captive, so that we serve not under the old written code but in the new life of the Spirit (Rom 7:4-6).

What then shall we say? That the law is sin? By no means! Yet, if it had not been for the law, I should not have known sin. I should not have known what it is to covet if the law had not said, "You shall not covet." But sin, finding opportunity in the commandment, wrought in me all kinds of covetousness. Apart from the law sin lies dead. I was once alive apart from the law, but when the commandment came, sin revived and I died; the very commandment which promised life proved to be death for me. For sin, finding opportunity in the commandment, deceived me and by it killed me. So the law is holy, and the commandment is holy and just and good (Rom 7:7-12).

What role does the Jewish law play in God's plan for the world? Is the law good or evil? How does sin use the law to bring persons to death? Does Paul misunderstand the role of the law in Israel?

In the covenant with Moses and the Israelites at Sinai God made the law a prominent actor in the drama of salvation. In itself the law was good, just and holy, because it came from God, did not contradict God's promises, and was destined to lead the chosen people to life. But the law could not produce the intended results. It provided an external norm for what should be done, but failed to supply the interior power to do it. So sin and death used the law to enhance their power over Israel.

Sin co-opted the law, seduced it, and used it to bring the Jewish people to death. As the law came under sin's power, it began to provide an occasion for sin to exercise its power. When it forbade what people had considered indifferent, it began to provide an occasion for sin to exercise its power. It awakened their desire for forbidden fruit.

The law also served as a "moral informer" to give the Jews a deep awareness of how sin operates in their lives. It helped them understand moral disorder as rebellion against God. People did not have this awareness before the law, and in awakening it, the law unmasked the evil power of sin. Sin used the law as its tool, but in doing so sin revealed its true desire to lead all persons to death. Although it was sin's accomplice, the law remained holy and just and good. It should have brought life to the Jews, but it brought only condemnation and death.

Why did God permit the law to serve the cause of sin and death? In God's plan the law was meant to lead all Jews to salvation through faith in Jesus Christ. From Moses to Christ it served as a temporary "slave-attendant" to prepare Israel for Christ. A slave-attendant in the Hellenistic world accompanied school-age children to and from classes and supervised their studies. However, when they became mature enough, the children no longer needed such an attendant.

The law accompanied Israel, as an attendant and companion, to help the Jews grow mature enough to receive justification by faith in Jesus Christ. God did not intend that, because they could not observe its stipulations, the law should make them desperate. Rather, God gave Israel the law as a temporary measure to prepare them and guide them toward the maturity that they would need to hear the message of salvation in Christ and respond with an adult faith.

Although the law is "spiritual" and came from God, it did not resolve the tension that persons experienced in trying to obey its stipulations. For the Jews in their earthbound condition as "flesh" were alienated from God. They were dominated by sin and tied to the earth. They were drawn to a material existence and distracted from any consideration of God. Sin kept them in bondage, so that, even if they wanted to obey God's law, they lacked the power to do so: "For I delight in the law of God, in my inmost self, but I see in my members another law at war with the law of my mind and making me captive to the law of sin which dwells in my members" (Rom 7:22-23).

God's action in Jesus Christ crucified and risen marked the end of the law: "There is therefore now no condemnation for those who are in Christ Jesus. For the law of the Spirit of life in Christ Jesus has set me free from the law of sin and death" (Rom 8:1-2). Christ freed the Jews from the law and from the destructive power of sin and death. In their place God introduced the Spirit and the positive power of grace leading to life. No longer did salvation come to both Jews and Gentiles anymore through works of the law and the legalistic attitude fostered by the law but through openness to God's gift in Christ and the gratitude fostered by faith.

How could Paul, "a Pharisee of the Pharisees ... blameless before the law" (Phil 3:5-6), ever come to this view of the Mosaic law? Did he simply misunderstand the law? Paul may have slighted the covenant context in which God gave the law to Moses and the Israelites. For them the law did not demand a static or sterile perfectionism. It rather supposed a covenant relationship. God graced the chosen people, and the people accepted the invitation to live by God's law.

Paul may have depended on the Greek translation of the Hebrew Scriptures in which the word *covenant* was translated as *last will, testament*. The Greek "last will" colored the Hebrew "covenant" with the connotation that the law expressed God's will. This connotation supported the tendency to exploit the law with detailed, legalistic specifications. It obscured the covenant as an agreement or pact between persons. It failed to emphasize that observing the law was an opportunity to deepen that mutual relationship. Paul was preoccupied with the Mosaic law as the will of God to be carried out according to the Pharisaic system of interpretation.

Abraham—Faith in the Promise

> Abraham "believed God, and it was reckoned to him as righteousness." So you see that it is men of faith who are the sons of Abraham. And the Scripture, foreseeing that God would justify the Gentiles by faith, preached the Gospel beforehand to Abraham, saying, "In you shall all the nations be blessed." So, then, those who are men of faith are blessed with Abraham who had faith (Gal 3:6-9).

> What then shall we say about Abraham, our forefather according to the flesh? For if Abraham was justified by works, he has something to boast about, but not before God.... How then was it (righteousness) reckoned to him? Was it before or after he had been circumcised? It was not after, but before he was circumcised. He received circumcision as a sign or seal of the righteousness which he had by faith while he was still uncircumcised. The purpose was to make him the father of all who believe without being circumcised and who thus have righteousness reckoned to them, and likewise the father of the circumcised who are not merely circumcised but also follow the example of faith which our father Abraham had before he was circumcised (Rom 4:1-3, 10-12).

Abraham was a key figure in God's plan for the world. The Jews regularly cited him as righteous before God, because he was faithful when tested and kept covenant with God. God called him to journey from his father's house toward a promised land in which he would become a great nation and a blessing for all families of the earth (Gen

12:1-3). When Sarah bore him no children and they were both advanced in years, Abraham trusted God's promise that his descendants would be as numerous as the stars and that he would father a multitude of nations (Gen 15:5-6; 17:4-22).

When asked to cut himself off from those descendants, Abraham did not hesitate to sacrifice Isaac, his only son in whom the promises were to be fulfilled. God then renewed these promises: "I will indeed bless you, and I will multiply your descendants as the stars of heaven and as the sand which is on the seashore.... And by your descendants shall all of the earth bless themselves, because you have obeyed my voice" (Gen 22:17-18).

Paul focused on the fact that God reckoned Abraham as righteous *before* he had been tested or circumcised. He was righteous by faith, that is, by his trusting God's gracious promises. Abraham believed that his descendants would become a great nation, even though he did not see how he and Sarah in their great age could have offspring. God rewarded Abraham for the righteousness of his faith, not because of his works. Abraham would later obey God in accepting circumcision and in submitting to the test asked of him. But those works did not make him righteous. For God had already considered him righteous by faith. If Abraham had been justified by his works, he would have reason to boast. But since he had not earned his justification but received it as an undeserved grace, he had nothing to boast about before God.

Abraham is the father of all who live by faith. He models a faith that is available to both Jews and Gentiles. He carries God's promised blessing to all nations of the earth. Whoever wants to share in that blessing must receive it through Abraham or not receive it at all. God considered Abraham righteous by faith and not by works, so that he might be father to all subsequent generations.

Abraham's true descendants are not those who share his blood but those who share his faith in God. As descendants, they inherit the blessings that God promised to Abraham when he called him to journey to a promised land and Abraham responded with faith. He trusted that God would give him offspring, because God had always been faithful to a sinful world. All people, both Jews and Gentiles, participate in God's promises to Abraham insofar as they resemble him in being righteous by faith and not by works.

God's promises to Abraham were fulfilled in the death and resurrection of Jesus Christ. All nations, classes, and sexes are equal in Christ, and all share equally in the promises to Abraham: "And if you are Christ's, then you are Abraham's offspring, heirs according to the promise" (Gal 3:29). God promised Abraham that he would be the father of many nations. His descendants would be as numerous as the stars and the sand on the seashore, and through him all nations would be blessed.

In God's plan those promises continue in and through Jesus Christ crucified and raised from the dead. In the new age Jew and Gentile, slave and free, male and female—all are considered righteous before God by a faith that resembles Abraham's. Abraham remains father to all who trust the same God who now graces them in Jesus Christ.

Salvation for Gentiles and Jews

> They are Israelites, and to them belong the sonship, the glory, the covenants, the giving of the law, the worship, the promises; to them belong the patriarchs, and of their race, according to the flesh, is the Christ. God who is over all be blessed for ever. Amen (Rom 9:4-5).

> If you confess with your lips that Jesus is Lord and believe in your heart that God raised him from the dead, you will be saved.... For there is no distinction between Jew and Greek; the same Lord is Lord of all and bestows his riches upon all who call upon him (Rom 10:9, 12).

> So too at the present time there is a remnant, chosen by grace. But if it is by grace, it is no longer on the basis of works; otherwise grace would no longer be grace (Rom 11:5-6).

> So I ask, have they [Israel] stumbled so as to fall? By no means! But through their trespass salvation has come to the Gentiles, so as to make Israel jealous. Now if their trespass means riches for the world, and if their failure means riches for the Gentiles, how much more will their full inclusion mean! (Rom 11:11-12).

Israel has rejected the Messiah who was born of their race and sent to redeem them. What is their future in God's plan for the world? Will they persist in rejecting the Christ and remain separated from God's love? If God's promised blessing to Abraham and his descendants, a blessing that came to fruition in the death and resurrection of Christ, can be rejected by his blood descendants in Israel, what assurance can there be that God's promise won't fail for non-Jews?

Israel was privileged by God's promise to Abraham, and God prepared for the Christ within the chosen people. God graced them with privileges that established their prior right to salvation: adoption, covenants, law, worship, promises, patriarchs—even Jesus himself. In rejecting Jesus has not Israel thwarted God's plan and proved it to have failed? Not at all, since Israel existed more by God's continued election than by racial descent. Israel's history is not that of a race, but that of a choice made by God in the promise to Abraham that through Isaac all the nations would one day be blessed.

Israel has continued as a chosen people because of God's fidelity to that original choice, not because of their blood lines or their works. God did not start them out with the promise to Abraham and then abandon them to make their own way through history. God's plan has continued to be at work in the history of Israel. Those Jews who reject the Messiah cannot frustrate God's consistent choice of Israel. God's choice, not their biological descent, has shaped their destiny, and that destiny remains in God's hands. Although God may appear to have failed with the chosen people, God continues in fact to carry out the plan to save both Gentiles and Jews by choosing Jesus Christ as the instrument of salvation.

Christian faith means trusting God "in your heart" and acknowledging that trust in public confession "with your mouth." It means seeing God's hand in the events of Christ's death and resurrection, seeing that since God raised Jesus from the dead God can be trusted to deliver all creation from its bondage to death. Since this faith resembles that of Abraham, God offers it as a blessing to both Gentiles and Jews. God's purpose in calling Abraham is now achieved through faith in Jesus Christ.

Why then did Israel reject Jesus Christ? Israel's stumbling opened the way to salvation for the Gentiles. In preaching the Gospel the apostles did not turn to the Gentiles until Israel rejected their message of salvation. The fact that more Gentiles than Jews responded with faith and were baptized may have raised problems for the apostolic community in Jerusalem. But Israel's rejection was necessary for the apostles to focus on their mission to the Gentiles.

When Israel recognizes how they have rejected God's Messiah, and how the Gentiles have become God's chosen people by their faith, envy and jealousy will bring them back to their place in the new people of God. As Israel's temporary departure enriched the Gentiles, so their final return will enrich not only themselves but also the Gentiles. In that time one community of Gentiles and Jews will be bonded together in Christ and will keep their gaze fixed on their union with him at his final coming.

God's people resemble an olive tree (Rom 11:17-24). As its roots and natural branches are healthy, so Israel is holy because of its privileges as God's chosen people. Some natural branches have fallen off the olive tree, in that some Israelites have separated themselves from God's promises by rejecting Jesus Christ. Meanwhile, some wild branches with no claim on the tree have been grafted onto it. These branches are the Gentiles who have trusted God's salvation in Christ. When Israel joins the Gentiles as God's chosen people through faith in Jesus Christ, the natural branches that fell to the ground will be grafted onto the tree alongside the wild branches. In the end, the one olive tree will stand with some of its original branches, the wild branches that were grafted onto it, and the natural branches that fell off for a time but have been regrafted onto the tree. Such is God's gracious plan for saving Gentiles and Jews.

Paul's struggle to understand shows that God's plan must remain a mystery that cannot be fully penetrated. For God's ways are not our ways, nor are God's thoughts our thoughts. Attempts to figure out God's plan end in failure, since the most we can attain are glimpses of a purpose in the events of salvation history. But failure leads us to praise a God who is faithful in determining to save the world through Jesus Christ. Paul knew that well:

> Oh the depth of the riches and wisdom and knowledge of God! How unsearchable are his judgments and how inscrutable his ways! ... For from him and through him and to him are all things. To him be glory for ever. Amen (Rom 11:33, 36).

Against this large, historical canvas Paul found meaning and resolved the conflict between his convictions and his experience. He reaffirmed his faith in God's fidelity to Israel and to the Gentiles. He saw more clearly than ever that he must preach Jesus Christ to the Gentiles with great urgency, since their coming onstage must precede his own people's accepting salvation.

Jesus Christ, crucified and risen, stands at the turning point of God's plan for the world. In him a new age had begun which he will fully establish when he returns. In him the tide begun by Adam is reversed, and the power of sin to lead persons to death is conquered. In him the Jewish law has completed its work, and Gentiles and Jews are called to a righteousness by faith. In him the promises to Abraham are carried into the new age with blessings for all races, classes, and sexes, blessings for all the nations of the earth.

As it did for Paul, the search for meaning may lead us to a drama in which our tensions and conflicts are seen as part of a larger landscape than our immediate experience. That dramatic story can explain where we have come from, why we are here today, and how we might orient ourselves toward the future. Seeing our conflicts in the context of that much larger plan, that cosmic order, that historical drama, may not enable us to resolve the conflicts between our convictions and our experience of the widening gap between rich and poor, the threat of nuclear war, increasing violence, and new patterns in marriage and family life. Within this new context, we may still find the conflicts and tensions challenging. However, we may also discover that they now have meaning.

What might our story look like? It might resemble Paul's story in the questions to be addressed and also perhaps in the content to be included. It will draw on traditions that we have cherished as a people. It will recall past actions and events that continue to be significant and carry meaning. It will reinterpret those actions and events in the light of our present situation. In that interpretation, we will discover what living our Christian faith in today's world means.

Paul reinterpreted the apocalyptic ages to show that the new age had already begun with the death and resurrection of Christ, and that it will be completely established at his triumphant return. Let's ask ourselves some questions as Paul did.

■ How do we interpret the present age?
■ Do we despair about the course of history? Do we see it rushing toward a tragic holocaust? Do we choose not to think about it?
■ Do we still believe in God's power to lead us into a new age of greater justice and cooperation, harmony and peace? Will the new age transform the present age? Or will the two ages be in radical discontinuity?
■ What images carry our view of the present age and its relation to the future?
■ Does the death and resurrection of Christ have a role to play in our scenario?

Paul retold the story of Adam to show how he started the tide of evil in the world with sin the power behind the transgressions and with death the end result. Sin and death ravaged the world and exercised power over both Jews and Gentiles. Jesus Christ reversed that tide with the counterforce of grace that leads to life.

■ How do we explain the presence of evil in our present world?
■ Has sin regained its power to lead us to death?
■ Have sin and death resumed their roles in the drama of salvation?

■ Has Christ conquered sin and death for all time or only for his own
time?

Movies like the *Star Wars* trilogy, television dramas with their horrible
conflicts and life-death struggles, and increasing violence in sports all
suggest that we are fascinated with the battle between good and evil. *Star
Wars* portrays that battle in outer space as a struggle between the powers
at work in Darth Vader and Luke Skywalker. We are not always sure who
is winning at every moment, but we choose to hope that in the end Luke
will conquer Darth Vader, that is, the power of good will triumph over the
power of evil. *Star Wars* resembles Paul's story about the struggle between
Adam-sin-death and Christ-grace-life, and our fascination with *Star Wars*
suggests that we share Paul's search for the meaning of evil in our world
and the power by which it will finally be destroyed.

Paul's story explained how sin appropriated the Jewish law, that
good and holy institution in Israel, and used it to bring the Jewish people
to death. In the new age the law was no longer needed as a slave-
attendant, since salvation for both Jews and Gentiles now came by faith
in Jesus Christ.

■ How might we evaluate our religious institutions—law, structures of
power, liturgical practices, decision-making, access to ministry, attitudes toward different races, classes and sexes?
■ Are these institutions more life-giving than death-dealing?
■ Has sin coopted them to lead us to death?
■ Should we attempt to renew them, or should we dispense with them,
as Paul dispensed with the Jewish law?

Long-range patterns of simultaneous decline and growth have begun to influence how we think, feel and act about cherished institutions
in our society. Medical costs are rising to the point where many people
can no longer afford adequate care, and the threat of malpractice suits
is leading some doctors to an early retirement. At the same time, we are
creating new less expensive styles of medical care. Competition is stim-
ulating multi-national corporations to retool their plants with robots
rather than people, and we face the challenge of how to provide new
jobs for the otherwise chronically unemployed.

As we reflect on the fact that these institutions must change, we
experience deep sorrow, the need to mourn, and concern for the future.
When Paul preached that Jesus Christ marked the end of the law,
Christian Jews must also have grieved. Like those early Christians, let's
ask ourselves about what the changes in our society might mean.

■ What does change mean? Why has it happened?
■ What will our institutions look like in twenty years?
■ What institutions will still be in place?
■ Which ones will have been transformed or will have disappeared?

Paul recognized Abraham as the father of all those justified by faith in Jesus Christ, both Jews and Gentiles, and he also saw that God's promises to Abraham are carried to fulfillment in the new age through the death and resurrection of Jesus Christ.

■ Where do we find models of faith, fathers and mothers to whom we can turn for inspiration—Mother Teresa, Martin Luther King, Jr., Dorothy Day, Mahatma Gandhi?
■ What couples model our convictions about marriage and family lives?
■ What persons show us how to live our Christian faith in the routines of our everyday lives?
■ Who carries for us the promise of a better future, the dream of a time when we will live together in greater justice, harmony, and peace?

Campaign promises often carry the vision of America as a land of unlimited opportunity in which the present crises will be resolved and all will participate in the promised dream. Recently our national mood has been described as "feeling proud again" after the shame of an endless war in Southeast Asia and corruption in our highest political offices. America seems to have recovered her vision of a future with endless possibility, and she has recaptured the conviction that we can do anything. Those who share economic and political power find this optimistic promise fulfilled. Yet others who are in deep economic distress or feel powerless are unable to believe that the United States has unlimited opportunities for all. Paul found meaning in God's promise to Abraham because it included all nations, classes and sexes. When that promise came to fulfillment in and through Jesus Christ, salvation by faith was equally available to Jews and Gentiles, masters and slaves, men and women.

Our imaginations can enable us to envision alternatives to our present experience. If we never imagine a better world for ourselves and others, we will never work to create it. Paul imagined an olive tree that included Jews and Gentiles, and that image convinced him that his mission to the Gentiles was essential to God's plan. As it did for Paul, imagination can empower us to find the presence of God in our world, to see through our present conflicts and tensions, and to catch a glimpse of what God has planned for our world.

Paul imagined a scenario in which God remained faithful to Israel, even though they had rejected salvation in Christ.

■ How might we create a scenario in which our deepest convictions can be reconciled with the facts of our experience?
■ Will things get worse before they get better?
■ Can we imagine alternatives to our present living patterns?
■ Is there an olive tree in our future?

Paul's story sets forth a drama of universal significance in which we can participate to find meaning, purpose, and structure in our lives. It can inform and influence the stories we tell and retell, as individuals and communities, to interpret life and respond to its complexity. But we must be willing to put aside our values, powers, and stories, so that we might participate in Paul's story.

As we suspend our world view and let ourselves be drawn onto Paul's stage, we may begin to find that elements in his story strongly resemble elements in our story. At first we may have found that Paul sets his story in a strange and foreign land, but gradually we have begun to feel comfortable and at home. Other elements may rub against, challenge, or even shatter our world. Whatever the outcome, our willingness to interact with Paul shows our readiness to let his story inform, influence, and even reshape our view of the world. Within that interaction we might also be drawn into contact with the transcendent reality that we call God.

7

Individuals and
Communities in the New Age

What does the death and resurrection of Christ mean for individual believers and communities of faith? How are we to understand ourselves as Christians in the new age? How are we to live in the time between Christ's death and resurrection and his final coming in glory? Paul and his communities struggled with these questions, and we struggle with them today, since they concern our identity as Christians. Paul responded to them by teaching that Christians are to live creatively within tensions such as life and death, power and weakness, hope and despair. They are also to keep their balance between polarities such as flesh and spirit, already and not yet, unity and diversity. We now want to understand his teaching and see how it might strengthen our identity as believers and communities of faith.

Recall once again the stage scene with the cross in the center and behind it the men and women who act in God's plan for the world. We now let our attention be drawn to the persons gathered at the front of the cross. They look toward both the cross and the historical persons behind it with their backs toward us in the audience. As individuals, these men and women have accepted Paul's message about God's action in Jesus Christ, and they have formed communities of faith. Now they wonder how to understand their relationship with God and how they might discover God's continuing action in their lives.

In Paul's scenario the new age which began in Jesus Christ, stands in radical "either ... or" discontinuity with the old age which began in Adam. Christ reversed the tide created by Adam, and in him grace and life conquered sin and death. By his death and resurrection Christ won the victory, but only when he returns at the parousia will that victory be complete. In the meantime, Christians live in both the new age and the old age, that is, in the time when the two ages co-exist with each other. They are challenged to make their way within the tensions created by the overlapping of the two ages and to learn how to recognize the powers of each age at work in their lives.

Christians are already saved from the sin and death of the old age, and they already participate in the grace and life of the new age. But they are not yet fully saved from the old age, and they do not yet fully participate in the new age. Christians understand themselves as living within this "already ... not yet" tension, as they participate in God's action in Christ and wait for it to be completed.

Individual believers and communities of faith are to imagine themselves standing on a balance beam without falling to one side or the other, working to keep their balance in the tension between the two ends of the beam. We will now explore that balancing act in terms of the metaphors that Paul uses to describe what the cross effects. Later we will see how Paul would have us trace God's action in our lives through the Spirit.

What the Cross Effects

For Paul the cross is so overwhelming in its power that he must weave a rich tapestry of metaphors to express its meaning. Each metaphor throws distinct light on God's action in Jesus Christ. But no single metaphor nor all of the metaphors together can exhaust what that action means. God's love revealed in Jesus Christ crucified and risen remains an incomprehensible mystery. Paul can catch only partial glimpses of its meaning through metaphors from his religious and cultural traditions.

Paul often begins to develop one metaphor, then moves quickly to another, and ends up with still another. He freely associates one metaphor with another rather than follow a straight line, logical argument. He moves with such vigor that the metaphors do not always mediate all that he wants to communicate. At times they seem to crack in his hands, as music in Beethoven's hands and stone in Michelangelo's.

Paul expresses the meaning of God's action in Jesus Christ through metaphors about what it effects in those who believe. It effects "salvation," that is, it restores them to safety, health, and wholeness from a state of sin (2 Cor 7:10; Rom 1:16; 10:10; 13:11). God's action in Jesus Christ also effects "reconciliation," that is, it reestablishes their friendship with God after a long period of alienation (2 Cor 5:18-20; Rom 5:10-11). It also effects "freedom," that is, it gives those who believe new rights and attitudes that set them free from slavery to sin and death (Gal 5:1, 13). It also effects "justification," that is, it enables them to stand before God's tribunal as innocent, upright, and righteous (Gal 2:16; Rom 3:26-28; 4:25; 5:1, 8).

God's action in Christ also effects "sanctification," that is, it removes those who believe from the realm of evil and dedicates them to God (1 Cor 1:30; 6:11). It also effects "transformation," that is, it gradually reshapes them according to the glory in the face of Christ (2 Cor 3:18; Rom 12:2). It also effects a "new creation," that is, it creates a new life, a new humanity with Christ as the new Adam through his life-giving Spirit (Gal 6:15; 2 Cor 5:17; 1 Cor 15:45). Finally, God's action in Jesus Christ effects "redemption," that is, it ransoms those who believe from captivity to sin and death and returns them to their status as a new people of God (Rom 3:24).

Paul invites us to test these metaphors for what they might disclose about God's action in our lives. At first they may seem strange and foreign, since they originate in a distant Jewish-Hellenistic world. We may need to learn more about what they meant to Paul and his communities. But by letting the metaphors live in us and by remaining with the tension they create, we may gradually experience resemblances that transcend time and culture. We may discover what it means to say that God's action in Christ saves us from sin and death, reconciles us to God and to each other, makes us innocent before God's tribunal, frees us from the anxiety of the law, enables us to enjoy a new life in Christ. When we have lived with these metaphors, we will be able to decide which of them help us find meaning in our lives, which need to be reinterpreted, and which must be discarded as no longer meaningful.

Paul uses a tapestry of metaphors to express the meaning of the cross. He was content with metaphors that were imprecise and open to contrary interpretations. After Paul died, theologians began to tease his metaphors into logical patterns and gradually transformed them into more precise concepts. Around them would rage Reformation and post-Reformation debates. In weaving this tapestry, however, Paul could not have known how much reflection he would later stimulate nor how later generations would try to make him a systematic theologian.

New Creation

> If anyone is in Christ, he is a new creation; the old has passed away, behold, the new has come (2 Cor 5:17).

> For neither circumcision counts for anything, nor uncircumcision, but a new creation (Gal 6:15).

> Thus it is written, "The first man Adam became a living being"; the last Adam became a life-giving spirit (1 Cor 15:45).

God's action in Christ creates new life, a new humanity with Christ at its head. It marks a new beginning for all creation, a fresh start, because Christ the new Adam has reversed the damage done by the old Adam. Christ makes all things new, as if the human race were coming fresh again from the hand of the Creator without distinctions, such as circumcised and uncircumcised, Jew and Gentile. Sin and death prevailed in the old creation, but in the new creation grace and life reign supreme through the Spirit. The old creation has ended, and in its place a radically new creation has been established.

Paul draws this metaphor from Jewish traditions that saw no better way to express God's saving activity than to compare it to creation. The Christian life is a "new creation," because individuals and communities are "in Christ," that is, they are members of the body of Christ who was crucified and raised from the dead. Because they have put on Christ in baptism, they belong to Christ and have received the Spirit of Christ. So they are a new creation.

Because of the Christ event, Christians participate in a new existence that replaces the old creation. Paul does not speak of rebirth or re-creation, but rather of new creation to stress that God sent his Son into the old creation to replace it. When Christians live by the Spirit of Christ, the new has come and the old has passed away.

Can we believe that because of God's action in Christ we live in a new creation? When we look at the dark side of our world, we see much more destruction than creation. We seem to be destroying our land, our natural resources, and such cherished institutions as family life and basic trust between persons. We seem to live more in the old age of sin and death than in the new age of grace and life. Yet Paul tells us that the old has passed away and the new creation has come.

What might this mean for us? Are there signs that the new creation has already begun, that an aquarian age has dawned in which people are choosing to live differently? Social commentators are calling for new models in business, banking, the professions, and family life. Spiritual renewal programs invite persons to discover God's action within and to act for greater justice in their everyday life and work situations. We continue to live in the old age, but we also want to remember that Christ has made all things new, that grace and life still prevail over sin and death, and that the Spirit empowers us to live the new creation in our world.

Reconciliation

> All this is from God, who through Christ reconciled us
> to himself and gave us the ministry of reconciliation;
> that is, God was in Christ reconciling the world to

himself, not counting their trespasses against them, and entrusting to us the message of reconciliation. So we are ambassadors for Christ, God making his appeal through us. We beseech you on behalf of Christ, be reconciled to God (2 Cor 5:18-20).

For if while we were enemies we were reconciled to God by the death of his Son, much more, now that we are reconciled, shall we be saved by his life. Not only so, but we also rejoice in God through our Lord Jesus Christ, through whom we have now received our reconciliation (Rom 5:10-11).

Reconciliation suggests scenes in which persons who have been alienated from each other come together again to restore their friendship. They resume communication after a time in which it had been broken. They begin to enjoy the peace and harmony they once knew but had lost in the time of alienation, and they hope that their reconciliation will be permanent.

In Christ's death and resurrection, God reconciled humanity and the world to himself after a long period of alienation. In the old age men and women were at odds with God, and a climate of hostility existed between them. For under the power of sin and death all persons alienated themselves from God and stood in need of reconciliation. God took the initiative when he reconciled humanity to himself through the death and resurrection of Christ. That event restored friendship, love, and peace between God and the world.

When persons accept God's initiative through faith, they gain access to God and enjoy a renewed harmony with God. No longer alienated, they enter the realm of reconciliation. Formerly at enmity, they are now at one with God.

Paul sees God's reconciliation in Christ reaching out beyond human persons to embrace the whole world. It affects not only humanity's relationship to God, their transition from hostility to friendship, but it also establishes a new condition for the created universe. Creation had been subjected to futility because of sin and death. Now it has been reconciled to its Creator.

When Paul accepted God's invitation to reconciliation through faith in Christ, God gave him the ministry of reconciliation. His own words and actions were to mirror God's work in reconciling creation. So Paul invited Jews and Gentiles to be reconciled to God though the Gospel he preached. When tensions arose in his communities, he appealed to them to be reconciled to God, to accept again his Gospel, and to recognize him as God's ambassador of reconciliation.

Can we believe that in the Christ event we have been reconciled to God and given the ministry of reconciliation? Alienation seems more prevalent in our society. We are losing respect for each other, and mistrust is alienating us from each other. Doctors often fear malpractice suits as they operate on their patients, ruthless competition often isolates business people from each other, and increased crime prevents us from leaving anything in our locked automobiles. Forces in our society are alienating us in fear and suspicion more than reconciling us in peace and harmony.

Paul wants to convince us that God has taken the initiative to reconcile us to himself, that we are meant to live together in justice, harmony, and peace, and that we are called to be ambassadors of reconciliation in the midst of alienation. He invites us to let these realities inform and influence our lives, so that we might respond to our world with the power to imagine how we might work to reconcile those who are alienated.

Salvation

> For God has not destined us for wrath, but to obtain salvation through our Lord Jesus Christ, who died for us so that whether we wake or sleep we might live with him (1 Thes 5:9-10).

> For the word of the cross is folly to those who are perishing, but to us who are being saved it is the power of God.... It pleased God through the folly of what we preach to save those who believe (1 Cor 1:18, 21).

> For I am not ashamed of the Gospel: it is the power of God for salvation to everyone who has faith, to the Jew first and also to the Greek (Rom 1:16).

> For man believes with his heart and so is justified, and he confesses with his lips and so is saved.... For there is no distinction between Jew and Greek; the same Lord is Lord of all and bestows his riches upon all who call upon him. For "everyone who calls upon the name of the Lord will be saved" (Rom 10:10, 12-13).

> For salvation is nearer to us now than when we first believed (Rom 13:11).

> Therefore, my beloved, as you have always obeyed,
> so now, not only in my presence but much more in
> my absence, work out your own salvation with fear
> and trembling; for God is at work in you, both to will
> and to work for his good pleasure (Phil 2:12-13).

Salvation evokes the scene of rescuing persons from a narrow strait—physical dangers such as illness, violence and death, or spiritual dangers such as sin and corruption. Salvation means that such persons are delivered from danger, that they are restored to a condition of safety and health, and that they are enabled to grow without fear of such dangers in the future.

In the old age Jews and Gentiles were caught in the power of sin and death. God took the initiative in Christ to deliver them from that danger and restore them to safety and health. God removed the boundaries that had separated them from one another, as well as the boundaries between himself and sinful humanity. Since faith was the right response to this saving gift, persons of whatever race or background had equal access to salvation. God may have meant salvation first for the Jews, but God also intended that the Gentiles be saved.

Paul was convinced that his Gospel was not mere speculative wisdom but carried God's power to save all those who believed. It shattered their worlds to disclose a deeper truth about God's power and wisdom. Through the contradiction of a crucified Messiah and the tension it created in Jews and Gentiles alike, those who believed were invited into the mystery of God's power in the apparent weakness of a crucified Messiah. Whoever trusted Paul's message and believed in the God about whom he spoke were saved from the dangers that surrounded them—the power of sin and death.

Salvation, a dynamic reality, begun with Christ's death and resurrection, manifests itself in the present time through Paul's preaching, but will be complete only when Christ returns in glory. Although convinced that the final coming was near, Paul still urged individuals and communities to work out their salvation in fear and trembling. Salvation may have already been won in Christ. But in the time when the old and new ages still overlap, that is, in the time until the parousia, Christians are to remain in good relationship with each other and with God.

Can we believe that God's action in Jesus Christ rescued us from the dangers of sin and death and restored us to safety? Again, the daily news reminds us of the dangers that surround us with reports of homes that are burned, persons who are murdered, and natural disasters such as famine and earthquake. Endless talks between the United States and the Soviet Union keep us fearful of nuclear war, the ultimate danger. In a world that has become a global village, we are more conscious that we live in danger than that we have been saved.

Yet Paul wants to tell us that if we trust his message we have nothing to fear from those dangers, since they cannot ultimately destroy us. For those who believe, life has triumphed over death. Such faith enables them to make their way in the world, sensitive to the surrounding dangers but also convinced that the dangers cannot destroy them, since they cannot deprive them of life.

Justification

> We ourselves, who are Jews by birth and not Gentile sinners, yet who know that a man is not justified by works of the law but through faith in Jesus Christ, even we have believed in Christ Jesus, in order to be justified by faith in Christ, and not by works of the law, because by works of the law shall no one be justified.... I have been crucified with Christ; it is no longer I who live, but Christ who lives in me; and the life I now live in the flesh I live by faith in the Son of God, who loved me and gave himself for me (Gal 2:15-16, 19b-20).

> But now the righteousness of God has been manifested apart from the law, although the law and the prophets bear witness to it, the righteousness of God through faith in Jesus Christ for all who believe. For there is no distinction; since all have sinned and fall short of the glory of God, they are justified by his grace as a gift, through the redemption which is in Christ Jesus, whom God put forward as an expiation by his blood, to be received by faith. This was to show God's righteousness, because in his divine forbearance he had passed over former sins; it was to prove at the present time that he himself is righteous and that he justifies him who has faith in Jesus (Rom 3:21-26).

Justification happens in a courtroom when a judicial process issues a verdict of acquittal, that is, when a judge declares accused persons free of guilt. That action restores the accused and enables them to return to society and be accepted as innocent before the law and no longer suspected of crimes or misdemeanors. Condemnation is the opposite of justification.

As Paul understands it, "justification" also mirrors the covenant between God and Israel. God's righteousness is the quality by which, as Israel's judge, God condemns Israel for their sin or justifies them for observing the law. Related to covenant mercy, God's righteousness designates the favor toward Israel within that context of judgment.

Paul sees God's righteousness as a dynamic reality, the expression and exercise of divine power seeking to realize itself in action. It is revealed in and through Christ's death and resurrection, since in that action God reaches out to embrace the world, Jews and Gentiles alike, and to justify those who let themselves be drawn into his action by faith.

Paul develops this metaphor in his polemic about the law. Before his conversion, Paul, as a Pharisee, considered justification limited to Jews who achieved it through works of the law. After his conversion, Paul opposed such an attitude of self-righteousness and complacency based on external practices, since it denied justification to the Gentiles.

Paul turned the Pharisaic understanding of justification on its head by affirming that God's final judgment had already occurred in the death of Jesus of Nazareth. Furthermore, in that act of judgment God acquitted everyone—all races, classes, and sexes. All humanity had been under the power of sin, but now God has acquitted them all in Christ Jesus. Finally, God's act of justification was a sheer grace, an unmerited gift, without any payment in good deeds.

No one need come before God's judgment seat with achievements that merit a favorable verdict. Indeed no one can earn justification, since God graciously gives the verdict of acquittal to those who believe, that is, to those who hear Paul's message and receive it as an undeserved gift. They believe that they are not "justified by works of the law but through faith in Jesus Christ" (Gal 2:16).

The fact that Paul took justification from a judicial setting and applied it to God's action in Christ has raised questions and teased theologians into much thought. Does God merely declare that sinful humanity is innocent by some legal fiction? Does humanity remain in the power of sin? Or does God also transform humanity through the Christ event? Paul never considered these questions, and his letters do not yield clear answers.

Nevertheless, Paul does seem to say that justification places humanity in a state of innocence before God through association with God's action in Jesus Christ, through incorporation into Christ by faith and baptism. Christians are not only declared but also become righteous before God with a righteousness through faith in Christ.

Can we believe in a righteous God who continues to reach out in covenant love to embrace our world, and justifies us by faith in Christ? Many people see evil and suffering as signs that a wrathful God is punishing us for our sins. These people believe that Jesus went to his death to placate an angry God and that we must suffer now to pay God for our guilt. Such persons can hardly see what Paul sees in the Christ event, namely God's love for the world, the Son's love for humanity, and the profoundly mysterious connection between love and death.

Our world is geared to achievements. We must compete to earn what we get, and at times we don't get what we deserve. We work hard to earn our livelihood, to be recognized, to enjoy the extras in life. How can Paul say that justification is a gift that God gives freely to everyone? That we don't need to earn it by going to church or saying prayers or doing anything else? How can he say that all we have to do is receive the gift, open it, and take responsibility for using it well?

Paul tells us that our deeds do not earn our right relationship with God. God justifies us before we act, and our actions are how we respond to that gift. Paul opens up for us a world in which we are called to surrender our need to swim and begin to float, that is, begin to live without anxiety, fear and the need to achieve. Faith can encourage us to stand firm in God's love, no matter what might call us to mistrust it. Rooted in that love, we will find that responding to others with love is easier.

Liberation

> For freedom Christ has set us free; stand fast therefore, and do not submit again to a yoke of slavery.... For you were called to freedom, brethren; only do not use your freedom as an opportunity for the flesh, but through love be servants of one another. For the whole law is fulfilled in one word, "You shall love your neighbor as yourself" (Gal 5: 1, 13-14).

> There is therefore now no condemnation for those who are in Christ Jesus. For the law of the Spirit of life in Christ Jesus has set me free from the law of sin and death (Rom 8:1-2).

> For the creation waits with eager longing for the revealing of the sons of God; for the creation was subjected to futility, not of its own will but by the will of him who subjected it in hope; because the creation itself will be

set free from its bondage to decay and obtain the glorious
liberty of the children of God (Rom 8:19-21).

"Set free" describes slaves whose master has changed their status by
giving them the rights of free persons, and it also suggests persons held
captive in war or oppression who are redeemed and returned to their
families. In the Hellenistic world freeing a slave was often considered a
sacred action. The slave deposited the price of freedom at the god's temple
and was considered to have passed from his owner's protection to that of
the gods who guaranteed freedom.

The Hebrew Scriptures often depicted God in the role of Israel's
"redeemer," that is, God resembled the family member whose duty it was
to buy back relatives who had lost their freedom. Above all God freed the
Israelites from bondage in Egypt, brought them to safety through crossing
the Red Sea, and acquired them as a people through the covenant at Sinai.
God's actions in the exodus from Egypt served as a paradigm for Israel to
understand both how God would free them from exile in Babylon and how
God would act on their behalf in the end time.

Paul believed that the end time began with God's action in Christ
which set humanity free from slavery to sin, death, and the law. God had
bought back those who were under the law. Now they could be called
"slaves of Christ" (1 Cor 7:23), since they owed only to him the obedience
of faith. In him they were set free from the constraints of the old age, and
they were bound only to his law of love: "Love fully satisfies the law" (Rom
13:10).

By Christ's death and resurrection, God has set us free from any
slavery that would cause us to live in fear, and God has redeemed us for
spontaneity and freedom. So Christians who observe any of the old law
fall back into restrictions imposed from outside. Both Jews and Gentiles
have been redeemed from captivity to the law precisely so that they might
be free to live by the law of the Spirit.

Already set free from the old age and living by the Spirit of the new
age, Christians, indeed the whole of creation, still look forward to the final
act of redemption. Creation waits to be set free from its bondage to decay,
and Christians await the redemption of the body (Rom 8:21-23).

Can we believe that God's action in Jesus Christ has set us free from
slavery to sin and death and has ransomed us from that captivity? Many
persons in our world—male and female, wealthy and poor—find themselves enslaved to drugs or alcohol, to gambling or running, to sex or
overeating. Addiction is a painful, pathological relationship with a substance or behavior that alters their mood but also leaves them full of shame
and guilt. Can Paul's message of freedom have meaning for the addict?

Paul states that God has taken the initiative to set us free by the death and resurrection of Jesus Christ. We do not accomplish our own freedom, nor do we earn it. We recognize that we are powerless in our enslavement, and we trust the power of God, that higher power, at work in Christ. We open ourselves to receive it, and we cooperate with it for our liberation. Recovering addicts are asked to admit that they are powerless over the substance or behavior to which they are addicted, to come to believe that a Power greater than themselves can set them free from the addiction, and to decide to turn their lives over to the care of God. Paul shows that this is God's way to freedom from whatever enslaves us.

Paul understands those persons standing on stage in front of the cross as newly created, reconciled to God and to each other, saved from the danger of sin and death, justified by faith in Jesus Christ, set free from slavery and ransomed from captivity. He invites us to see ourselves in the same way by letting these rich metaphors gradually disclose both the meaning of the cross and how we are to understand ourselves as Christians in our world.

Tracing the Spirit

In this scene Paul also describes how the Christians gathered around the cross can live their faith in the world and discover God's action in their lives. Baptized into Christ's death and resurrection and looking forward to his return in glory, they are now to live within the tension created by their being in both the old age and the new.

Within that tension Christians are to live by the grace they have received, and they are not to fall back into slavery to sin. Newly created, reconciled to God, saved from danger, justified by faith, set free from the law, they must now live and be guided by the Spirit. For their human spirit is not isolated from the divine Spirit that dwells within them, nor does that divine Spirit work independently on their human spirit. Christians have received the Spirit as an undeserved gift, but they are obliged to trace how that Spirit acts in their lives.

Tracing a bird in flight means tracking how it moves across the sky. Tracing a theme in a musical composition means listening attentively to how it is introduced, repeated, and developed. Tracing how young people grow means charting their physical, social, psychological, and intellectual development. Paul urges Christians to trace how the Spirit acts in their lives by learning how to recognize its presence and follow its promptings.

As God's gift, the Spirit both signifies that the new age has dawned and points to its future completion. The Spirit resembles a down-payment, that is, the money paid now to indicate that the buyer will deliver the rest as soon as possible. God has given the Spirit to indicate that the new age will soon be established in its fullness (2 Cor 1:22). The Spirit also resembles the first-fruits that announce an abundant crop soon to be harvested. In enabling Christians to live by the Spirit, God has announced a rich harvest to come when the new age has finally been established. Christians now celebrate the Spirit, as the power by which they are to live until their Lord returns, and they also look forward in hope to that final consummation.

According to Paul, "flesh" is the domain of power in which sin and death can still operate, because the old age has not yet ended. Flesh refers to the entire person in its weak, transitory, unreliable character. It does not refer to a lower nature at odds with a higher nature in the human person, nor does it suggest an inner struggle between body and soul. For Paul did not dichotomize the human person into lower and higher nature nor into body and soul.

As the ally of sin, flesh can still lead individual believers and faith communities to death, whereas spirit is the power through which grace can lead them to life with God. Spirit always wins the struggle against flesh, because God won the decisive victory over sin in Christ's death and resurrection. However, in the overlapping ages Christians can expect to struggle between flesh and spirit, and they can expect to live within its tension.

So Christians are to trace the Spirit already given but not yet fully given, and they are to resist the flesh already conquered but not yet fully conquered. Living within this unavoidable tension will be death-dealing, if they let flesh enslave them, but life-giving insofar as they are guided by the spirit.

Other polarities describe the same tension: "... the spirit of the man which is in him ... the Spirit of God ... the spirit of the world ... the Spirit which is from God (1 Cor 2:11-12) ... the dispensation of death ... the dispensation of the spirit (2 Cor 3:7-11) ... the law of God in my inmost self ... the law of sin in my members (Rom 7:14, 25) ... you are not in darkness ... you are all sons of light ... night ... day" (1 Thes 5:4-5).

Since Paul inherits a very fluid notion of personality from his Jewish heritage, he is not always clear about how the Spirit is related to Christ. Sometimes he seems to identify them by interchanging "Spirit of God," "the Spirit of Christ," "Christ," and "the Spirit of him who raised Jesus from the dead" to describe how God dwells in the Christian (Rom 8:9-11). Paul even goes so far as to say: "Now the Lord is the Spirit, and where the Spirit of the Lord is, there is freedom" (2 Cor 3:17).

Elsewhere Paul parallels God (or the Father), Christ (or the Son), and the Spirit in a way that would later lead to doctrinal statements about the Trinity: "The grace of the Lord Jesus Christ and the love of God and the fellowship of the Holy Spirit be with you all" (2 Cor 13:14). We must let Paul speak from his non-technical perspective, and we must listen without imposing on him later, more technical refinements of person, nature, and substance.

Paul describes the Spirit's role in God's action in Christ. Christ opened the way to a new life in union with his death and resurrection. The Spirit enables individuals and communities to live out that life for God in Christ. The Spirit empowers Paul in his preaching (1 Cor 2:4) and the Christians in their faith, hope, and love (Rom 15:13). The Spirit frees both Jew and Gentile from the law (Gal 5:18), from the cravings of the flesh (Gal 5:16), and from all immoral conduct (Gal 5:19-24).

The Spirit dwells in the Christians (Rom 8:9-11), empowers them to be children of God (Gal 4:6; Rom 8:14), assists them in prayer when they are too weak to pray (Rom 8:26), and keeps them aware of their relation to the Father (Rom 8:14-17). The Spirit is identified with Jesus Christ as the power within the Christians: "But you were washed, you were sanctified, you were justified in the name of the Lord Jesus Christ and in the Spirit of our God" (1 Cor 6:11). Christians received this power in baptism as an undeserved gift, and now they are called to give up their own power, so that they might live out of the power that is Christ and his Spirit.

Paul frequently refers to tracing the Spirit: "Do not quench the Spirit, do not despise prophesying, but test everything; hold fast what is good, abstain from every form of evil" (1 Thes 5:19-22). Christian love should yield a rich harvest of true knowledge, so that the community might test what is worthwhile (Phil 1:9-10). Communities are to let their minds be transformed, so that they can test what is of God (Rom 12:2).

Paul regards discernment as a special gift of the Spirit. It includes the spiritual sensitivity to distinguish true from false prophecy: "Let two or three prophets speak, and let the others weigh what is said.... For God is not a God of confusion but of peace" (1 Cor 14:29, 33). This gift is given to mature Christians who are attuned to the Spirit (1 Cor 2:14-16), and it demands that they align themselves with the mind of Christ bestowed by the Spirit.

Paul recognizes, however, that all Christians are called to trace the action of the Spirit in their everyday lives. All individuals and communities are expected to live according to the Spirit, and all will be judged on the last day (1 Cor 3:10-13). Diligence in tracing the Spirit enables them to cope with the ambiguity in their present struggle between flesh and spirit and to look forward with hope to that day of judgment.

How can Christians know that they are living by the Spirit? Paul develops the following criteria: if their actions are consistent with the mystery of the cross, if they continue to grow in faith, hope and love, if they experience the fruit of the Spirit, and if they build up the community as the body of Christ.

Consistent with the Cross

In tracing the Spirit, Christians begin with the cross at center stage, never let it out of their sight, and return to it often for confirmation. As we have seen, the cross represents God's saving action in Christ crucified and risen, and it reveals the paradox of God's power in human weakness and God's wisdom in human foolishness. Through faith and baptism, Christians are united to that mystery, absorbed and incorporated into its paradox, and assimilated to the death and resurrection of Christ. They share his sufferings, become like him in his death, and experience the power of his resurrection.

Christians can expect that the Spirit's action in their lives will reflect this mysterious paradox. The Spirit will be disclosed to individuals and communities when they discover that paradox at work in their lives, when they learn to have compassion on and find strength within their weakness, when their pain leads them to new possibilities.

Paul models this dynamic process when he recognizes in his own suffering that he participates in the death of Christ and witnesses to the power of his resurrection (2 Cor 4:7-11). Suffering taught him that he was a weak earthen vessel, but faith enabled him to trace the Spirit at work to reveal within him the pattern of Christ's death and resurrection.

The Spirit also works in suffering that calls forth the capacity to endure, the endurance that over time strengthens character, and the character that enables believers to hope, that is, to choose life in their death-like situation (Rom 5:3-5). Christians can be sure that this process will not disappoint them, since it is grounded in the love of God revealed in the cross and poured into their hearts by the Spirit.

Faith-Hope-Love

God's action in Christ enables Christians to have faith, live in hope, and love each other and God. These gifts identify and define the Christian community. Paul thanks God for them, and he invites his communities to appreciate and cultivate them. He writes to the Thessalonians: "We give thanks to God always for you all, constantly mentioning you in our prayers, remembering before our God and Father your work of faith and labor of love and steadfastness of hope in our Lord Jesus Christ" (1 Thes 1:2-3).

As we have seen, faith means that Christians are willing to hear Paul's message about the cross and respond to its call. It means that they let go of previous understandings so as to reach out for the mystery of Christ's death and resurrection. It means that they trust Paul enough to let his message begin to inform and influence their lives, and that they trust the God about whom he spoke and the Jesus who died and was raised from the dead. Finally, it means that they open themselves to receive God's love as an undeserved gift.

We have also seen that hope means that Christians have the freedom and power to choose life even in death-like situations. It lifts them out of the clutches of pain and enables them to see in the pain the seeds of new possibilities. Christian hope is grounded in God's unconditional love, revealed in the cross of Jesus Christ, and communicated by the Spirit.

Through his death and resurrection, Jesus has set Christians free to live according to his law of love: "For in Christ Jesus neither circumcision nor uncircumcision is of any avail, but faith working through love" (Gal 5:6). Faith grounds the Christian life, and love makes it a reality. Though distinct from each other, they cannot be separated. Faith makes love possible, and love translates faith into action. Christians have been freed from the law precisely to serve each other: "For the whole law is fulfilled in one word, 'You shall love your neighbor as yourself' " (Gal 5:14).

Paul explains what love entails in a beautiful hymn (1 Cor 13). Love is the attitude that most reveals the action of the Spirit. Gifts such as speaking in tongues, prophesying, understanding, and generous self-giving have no value unless they are informed by love. Love can be imagined as a person who shows patience and kindness to others, who refuses to be jealous or boastful, arrogant or rude, who bears and believes all things, hopes and endures all things. Since it depends on faith and provides grounds for hope, love is the clearest sign that the Spirit is present and active in individuals and communities: "So faith, hope, love abide, these three; but the greatest of these is love" (1 Cor 13:13).

Fruit of the Spirit

Paul describes Christians as those in whom the Spirit is free to bear fruit. That fruit is not to be confused with virtues that Christians can select and cultivate on their own, nor with qualities of personal behavior which they can develop, nor with good deeds that constitute a new law code. The fruit of the Spirit is a package of benefits that comes with the gift of the Spirit. Christians receive the Spirit as the source from which the fruit can grow and develop. Since the fruit has not been given with the Spirit, Christians cannot claim to possess it. Rather, as they live by the Spirit, they will come to know the delectable fruit that the Spirit produces with their active involvement.

Paul contrasts the fruit of the Spirit to the works of the flesh: "But the fruit of the Spirit is love, joy, peace, patience, kindness, goodness, faithfulness, gentleness, self-control; against such there is no law" (Gal 5:22-23). When Christians find this fruit in their lives, they know that they are living by the Spirit and not falling into the domain of the flesh.

Paul knew that individual believers and communities fell short of bearing such fruit in their everyday lives. Pettiness often led them to quarrel with each other, outside influences made them question Paul's authority and message, and factions often divided communities on important issues. Paul still proclaimed this vision of what they were meant to become and constantly urged them to live by the Spirit: "If we live by the Spirit, let us also walk by the Spirit. Let us have no self-conceit, no provoking of one another, no envy of one another" (Gal 5:25-26).

Building up the Community

Christian communities trying to live by the Spirit must strike a balance between a strong unity and a rich diversity. They should remember that they resemble a human body: "For as in one body we have many members, and all the members do not have the same function, so we, though many, are one body in Christ and individually members of one another" (Rom 12:4-5). Their unity must not be reduced to uniformity and must allow for and even stress their diversity. For all who profess that Jesus is Lord have received the one Spirit of God who moves them to share their gifts in love for each other. Christians must discover their different gifts and with them build up the community as the body of Christ.

Christians build up the body of Christ when they share the Lord's supper. It was instituted as a common meal to express unity and solidarity, but some Corinthians had destroyed its meaning through their lack of concern for poor members (1 Cor 11:17-34). Since their selfish indifference was damaging rather than building up the community, Paul invites them to eat their meal at home rather than pretend a unity that did not exist. Love and care for each other were an essential condition for the Eucharist to have any meaning. If they could not live according to what they celebrated, they might better refrain from the celebration.

Christians also support one another by how they behave at a dinner party (1 Cor 8:1-13; 10:23-31). The Corinthians disputed among themselves about eating meat that may have been sacrificed to pagan idols. Some thought that eating the meat was all right and laughed at others who worried that it might be wrong. Paul insists on their freedom in Christ to attend marriages and funerals and to eat the meat provided, whether or not it had been offered to idols. But he also asserts that stronger members of the community are not to scandalize weaker members. Building up the community was more important than exercising freedom: "Therefore, if food is a cause of my brother's falling, I will never eat meat, lest I cause my brother to fall" (1 Cor 8:13).

Worship in Corinth provides another example of tracing the Spirit at work in building up the community (1 Cor 12-14). Some members spoke out loud in tongues and lorded it over the others whom they considered less gifted. Paul responds that the value of the Spirit's gifts is to be determined by how much they contribute to building up the community as the body of Christ (1 Cor 14:1-5). Whoever prophesies speaks to the entire community for their encouragement, and everyone understands what is said. But whoever speaks in tongues utters mysteries that no one understands. Paul says of himself: "I thank God that I speak in tongues more than you all; nevertheless, in church I would rather speak five words with my mind, in order to instruct others, than ten thousand words in a tongue" (1 Cor 14:18-19).

We Christians still struggle to trace the Spirit in our lives, as we try to keep our balance between being already saved by Christ's death and resurrection and being not yet fully saved. Paul cannot tell us how to act nor give us clear-cut principles for action. He can, however, guide us in tracing the Spirit, as he guided the communities he founded. His message discloses a vision of life from which flow attitudes and values that can inform and influence us as individuals and communities. We can make them our own by letting them into the fabric of our lives, as we take responsibility for discovering the Spirit at work in our unique, historical situation.

After struggling for five years, a wife and husband wonder about ending their almost intolerable marriage with its mutual destruction. What might divorce do to them and their children? Church rules and regulations do not work as well as in the past, nor do they provide answers to their complex issues.

Paul might ask such a couple to look toward the cross. Must their pain lead to death? Is their situation beyond hope, that is, beyond choosing life in apparent death? Can they imagine the paradox that in their weakness they might experience a new power, God's power at work to lead them to a new life together? Paul might give them a new perspective from which to reflect on their situation, but he cannot provide them with answers.

Christian men and women often want to be true to their religious values in their work situations, but they hesitate for fear of what that might entail. How are they to make their way in a world with different values? How can they risk losing what they have worked hard to attain for themselves and their families? Tensions between work and religion, between the secular and the sacred, between faith and life, lead them to ask how to find the Spirit in the marketplace and discover what is right in their everyday lives.

Paul might ask them to reflect on how faith, hope, and love inform and influence their actions. Are they open to the gift of God's love and to living by the power of the Spirit? Are they convinced that in what can seem to be dangerous risks may lie the seeds of new opportunities? What do their faith and hope enable them to do in their concrete situation? What does their love of others prompt them to do? Paul might also ask whether they live with more peace than anxiety, more kindness than irritability, more joy than sadness, more love than hatred. For the climate in their lives can disclose whether they are living by the Spirit or by the flesh.

A midwest parish exploded three years ago when the struggle between the pastor and the coordinator for adult religious education could no longer be repressed. The explosion caused a chain reaction in which long-standing tensions suddenly surfaced. The coordinator resigned, staff members were divided among themselves, and the parishioners expressed their frustrations. Long months of hard work have been needed to rebuild the parish. The people have wondered if the Spirit was working in their conflict and how to remain open to the Spirit.

Paul would urge them, as he did his communities, to recover their sense of unity and let go of the divisions that almost destroyed them. He would suggest that they call forth the different gifts of the parishioners, and that they make only those decisions that have the chance of rebuilding their parish community. For the Spirit can teach them how their conflicts can contribute to their growth as the body of Christ.

Take a few minutes to let your mind wander over what you have just read. Then ask yourself:

- Is there any way in which the cross stands at center stage in your life?
- What helps you to trust in God's love?
- What keeps you from trusting in God's love? What holds you back from accepting that gracious gift?
- When have you been aware of the fruit of the Spirit permeating your life, working in your life?
- What image do you have of yourself as a follower of Christ, renewed in the Spirit?

Part III

PRAYING WITH PAUL'S LETTERS

When we pray, we may say formal prayers such as grace at meals and morning or night prayers. We may pray together in church on Sundays or at devotions during the week. We may pray privately at home or in church. We may meet God in a beautiful sunrise or in the roaring sea. As we drive to work or home from the supermarket, we may reflect on God's action in our everyday lives. We use different styles of prayer. We pray at any time, in any place.

However varied the times and places, we desire to encounter God in love. Prayer is a place for that encounter. Prayer arises from our deepest desire to know and love God and to be known and loved by God. It expresses our belief that God wants to reach out and speak to us. It is born in our need to be with God. God wants to share life with us. God calls us; God empowers us to respond.

Prayer demands that we set other concerns aside to spend focused time with God. God is present and active in all the events of our lives. The more real God is for us, the more we need time alone together so that our relationship might grow. In this time we listen for God and respond with mind and heart.

Dialogue with God is a pure gift. We cannot achieve it by our own efforts. God gifts us to want to pray, invites us to pray, and enables us to respond freely in prayer. Gratitude, then, is a basic attitude that permeates our prayer. It quiets us and opens us to the reality of God in our lives.

At times we pray with Scripture. We approach the biblical text with the faith conviction that God wants to meet us in and through this word. Scripture is a privileged place to encounter God. Scripture resembles the curtain at a stage play. It opens us to contact with God, just as the curtain opens us to contact with the people on stage. Scripture also resembles a diving board. It springs us into communication with God,

just as the board springs divers into their complex gyrations in the air.
The board enables the divers to perform, just as Scripture enables us to
communicate with God. Once we are in communication, we can forget
about the Scripture. Like the diving board, it has served its purpose in
our prayer. The point in prayer is to communicate with God, encountering
God in love.

When we study Scripture, we want to understand it and find meaning
in its message. When we pray with Scripture, we use it as a privileged
means through which we hope to encounter God in love. Praying with
Scripture awakens our desire to study, and studying Scripture enriches
our prayer.

In praying with the Gospels, we relate to stories about how Jesus
preached and taught, how he healed the sick and cast out demons, how
he spoke in parables and instructed his followers, how he shared his
work with his disciples, how he won the debates with his enemies, how
he suffered and died, how he rose from the dead and will return in
triumph. We may simply read and listen to these stories, and as we do
so listen also for the Lord. Or after reading and rereading a particular
episode, we might ask questions about it and gradually move to encounter
Jesus in prayer. Or we might recreate the scene in our imagination and
let ourselves be drawn into what the persons are saying and doing.
However we choose to pray, the Gospels provide us with immediate
access to Jesus and his followers.

In his letters Paul makes statements about dying and rising in
Christ, about God's plan for the world, about individuals and communities
in the new age. His statements are rich in symbols and metaphors, but
they do not describe scenes from the earthly life of Jesus. Instead, they
rivet our attention on the crucified and risen Lord. In statement after
statement Paul tells us what Jesus' death and resurrection can mean to
those who believe in him.

If we approach Paul's letters expecting them to be like the Gospels,
we will be disappointed and frustrated. Methods that work well in praying
with the Gospels may not work at all when we pray with Paul's letters.
So, why should we pray with Paul? What can Paul contribute to our
prayer life? First of all, Paul models prayer, and we can learn from his
example. He models prayer above all in his experience of the risen Lord.
In general he remains reticent about his prayer life. But we catch glimpses
of it in his visions and revelations, in his personal prayer to be delivered
from the thorn in his flesh.

Second, Paul talks about prayer, and we can learn from what he
says. For him, prayer is focused on the mystery of Jesus Christ, and he
sees himself as the steward of that mystery. Prayer also reflects on the

mystery of the human person. It is the place where God's power encounters human weakness, where we know ourselves as God's children.

Third, Paul includes prayers in his letters, and we can use them for prayer. Paul often praises God for his glory and power, gives thanks to him, and expresses wishes, hopes and dreams. These prayers reveal how Paul worked to establish a deeply prayerful relationship with his communities. They can teach us how to maintain the same spirit in our lives.

Lastly, prayer can be the setting in which we both dialogue with Paul and find meaning in his message. We have explored these two activities. We can pursue them in study, and we can bring them to prayer. In prayer we perform them as a means to encounter God. We accept Paul's letters as God's inspired word, that is, as a privileged place where we can communicate with God. We listen to Paul's statements about God's action in Christ and let them live in us so that they may disclose the presence of that transcendent reality we call God.

We have dialogued with Paul and found meaning in his message. Now we want to see what praying with Paul's letters means. How can dialoguing and finding meaning lead us to encounter God? When we dialogued with Paul, we looked for resemblances between his life experiences and ours. When we found meaning in his message, we let ourselves interact with his view of life. Now, we desire that, as the inspired word of God, Paul's letters disclose to us the hidden, mysterious, transcendent God and Jesus Christ his Son and our Lord.

In this section we will learn from Paul's practice of prayer. We will listen to what he says about prayer, and we will grow familiar with the prayers in his letters (Chapter Eight). We will then describe cases and methods appropriate to praying with his letters (Chapter Nine).

Before moving on, I invite you to reflect on what prayer means to you. In answering the following questions you will find words to name your experience. You might want to begin to answer them now and return to them again as you focus on praying with Paul's letters.

- What surfaces in you when you hear the word prayer?
- When, where, and how do you pray?
- What did "they" tell you about prayer? What has your life experience told you?
- What do you want prayer to be in your life?
- Can you remember a positive experience of praying with Paul's letters? What made it positive?
- Can you remember a negative experience of praying with Paul's letters? Why was it negative?
- Do you want to pray with Paul's letters? If so, why? If not, why not?

8

Paul and Prayer

"**R**ejoice always, pray constantly, give thanks in all circumstances, for this is the will of God in Christ Jesus for you" (1 Thes 5:16-18). With these words Paul discloses how he sees prayer as the center of the Christian life. He begins each letter with a prayerful greeting and ends it with a benediction. Though generally reticent, Paul does give a few examples of his own prayer life. In his letters we find samples of the prayers he cherished. We want to see what Paul might contribute to our understanding of prayer. We will look at him as a man of prayer, at how he viewed prayer, and at the prayers in his letters.

As a man of his times, tradition, and culture Paul used exclusively masculine images for God. He prayed to God as "Father" and invited Christians to do the same. For to do otherwise would have meant stepping out of his culture. Had he been living in today's world, he would have used more inclusive imagery and language for God. In this chapter, I have chosen to stay with Paul's imagery and with the masculine pronoun for God. As you read these pages, I urge you to make whatever adjustments might be needed to help you appreciate Paul's view of prayer. In the Appendix, "Paul and Women," I will argue that, while using masculine imagery for God, Paul is the clearest voice in the New Testament for the radical equality of men and women.

Man of Prayer

Paul's prayer was first that of a Jew accustomed to the sabbath observances in the synagogue at Tarsus and later to the feasts in Jerusalem. He was also familiar with the personal prayer of any religious man in Israel. As a youth, Paul would have learned to sing the psalms and recite the Shema, the traditional formula of Jewish faith (Dt 6:4-9). As a student in Jerusalem, he would have studied the Hebrew Scripture, mastered the rabbinic style of interpretation, and come to value prayer in his life as a Pharisee.

Paul's experience of the risen Lord transformed his attitudes toward prayer. He continued to worship and serve the same God of Israel. But Jesus Christ replaced the law as the center of his communication with God. God revealed his Son to Paul, Paul saw the Lord, and the risen Lord appeared to him. Paul does not tell us how the revelation happened, whether he saw a vision or heard a voice, whether God communicated to him with or without words. He is content to say that in this experience God gave him a deep, personal, even mystical, knowledge of Jesus Christ. Paul was enabled to accept the gift in faith.

In that experience God revealed himself to be above all "the Father of our Lord Jesus Christ." This image of God might have struck Paul's contemporaries as irreverent. But Paul realized that the Father had been pleased to set him apart from the womb. God called Paul to faith in the Son and sent Paul to preach that Son to the Gentiles. Paul recognized that all initiative belonged to the Father, a recognition that profoundly transformed his prayer.

God also revealed himself to be "our Father." We are "children" of God through being incorporated into the Son. As a result, we Christians direct our prayer in the Son to the Father by the power of the Spirit. In prayer we grow more deeply aware of being "children" of this loving Father.

At the center of Paul's inner life and at the heart of his prayer was Jesus Christ. He lived within Paul, and he enabled Paul to participate in his death and resurrection. Paul continually turned to the Christ within, as the power by which he now lived (Gal 2:19-20). In fact, he is related to God the Father, since he is incorporated into, assimilated into, baptized into the Son. Prayer often meant becoming more aware of that union, trusting in Christ's power rather than his own, and letting himself be led by the Spirit.

Paul abandons his customary reticence to describe two experiences in prayer, the visions and revelations he enjoyed and his request to be delivered from a "thorn in the flesh."

> I must boast; there is nothing to be gained by it, but I will go on to visions and revelations of the Lord. I know a man in Christ who fourteen years ago was caught up to the third heaven, whether in the body or out of the body I do not know, God knows. And I know that this man was caught up into Paradise—whether in the body or out of the body I do not know, God knows—and he heard many things that cannot be told, which man may not utter (2 Cor 12:1-4).

And to keep me from being too elated by the abundance
of revelations, a thorn was given me in the flesh, a
messenger of Satan, to harass me, to keep me from
being too elated. Three times I besought the Lord about
this, that it should leave me; but he said to me, "My
grace is sufficient for you, for my power is made perfect
in weakness." I will all the more gladly boast of my
weaknesses, that the power of Christ may rest upon me
(2 Cor 12:7-9).

Paul first describes the vision that made him more profoundly aware
of the mystery in God. Again he tells us nothing of what he saw or
heard. He simply refers to it as a revelation. It resembled an ascension,
because it gave Paul direct knowledge of his Lord's glorification.

Why did Paul tantalize us by mentioning this experience but not
describing its content? He could have said nothing about it. Paul wasn't
exactly modest by temperament. Nor does he seem afraid that his boasting
might be taken as arrogance. Perhaps he simply wanted to convey his
deep sense of the mystery in which all prayer participates, the mystery
of God as Father freely offering to share life with us, as children in the
Son Jesus Christ.

Paul then prayed to be delivered from a "thorn in the flesh." The
thorn may refer to persecution or sexual desire, but it most likely designates
a disease that Jews commonly believed to be caused by Satan. Paul
prayed not to God but to the risen Lord. He made his request with great
urgency, because he and his missionary work were under severe attack.
Opponents were challenging his right to call himself an apostle and
discrediting his message about freedom from the law.

Paul prayed with confidence that the Lord would deliver him from
the disease that further crippled him. Christ's answer went beyond and
even contradicted his prayer. The Lord did not cure the disease, but
rather disclosed its value and meaning. Paul's prayer made him aware
that perseverance in prayer carries infallible efficacy. As he continued
to pray, Paul realized that the thorn in the flesh was meant to teach him
how to ground his trust more firmly in God. His physical weakness
showed him how he was to depend more radically on God's power in
Jesus Christ, a power that can operate through such weakness.

In these texts we can catch glimpses of Paul the man of prayer. His
experience of the risen Lord shaped his prayer. He knew God to be his
Father and himself to be one with his God's Son Jesus Christ. Paul's
visions and revelations, as well as his plea to be delivered from the thorn
in his flesh, show us the richness of Paul's personal prayer. What can

we learn from Paul? Our prayer, like his, must arise out of what is rich in our lives. We must cherish those images of God that speak most to our experiences and lead us to find meaning in them. They may resemble the masculine images that Paul found meaningful. Or they may be quite different. Paul does not ask us to pray as he prayed, but he does teach us to trust our experience as the place to encounter God in prayer.

Pauline Prayer

Prayer, as Paul understands it, focuses on the mystery of God's action in Jesus Christ. God initiated the action. It took place in the death and resurrection of Jesus Christ. Individuals and communities begin to participate in that action through faith and baptism, and they continue their participation through personal and communal prayer in the Spirit.

Prayer is most often addressed to God, as "the Father of our Lord Jesus Christ" (Rom 15:6). We called God "Abba," an intimate term that is better translated "Daddy" than "Father." We can use this familiar term, since God has made us his children: "And because you are sons, God has sent the Spirit of his Son into our hearts, crying, 'Abba! Father!' " (Gal 4:6).

Jesus Christ died and was raised, sits at God's right hand and intercedes for believers, and will return in triumph. Prayer may sometimes be addressed to Christ. But it continues through him to the Father. It is more often directed to the Father in the name of Christ. Jesus Christ is more the power by which Paul prayed to the Father than the person he addressed in prayer.

The Spirit empowers us to dialogue with the Father through the Son. The Spirit is given, so that we may know that God has made us children (1 Cor 2:12). The Spirit leads us in our weakness: "Likewise the Spirit helps us in our weakness; for we do not know how to pray as we ought, but the Spirit himself intercedes for us with sighs too deep for words" (Rom 8:26).

In prayer we also confront the mystery of the human person, since it is the setting where God's power encounters human weakness. We know the agony of prayer in weakness. We experience God's power in Jesus Christ our Lord. We respond with gratitude for such an undeserved gift. In our individual and communal prayer we are invited to acknowledge our weakness, surrender to God's power, center our lives on God's unconditional love, and allow God's power to inform our lives.

Prayer is informed by faith in the mystery of God's action in Christ, by hope learned through suffering, and by love poured out into our hearts by the Holy Spirit. In faith we have been opened to receive God's love as a pure gift. Through baptism we have been incorporated into Christ. Suffering has taught endurance and through endurance we learned hope. We have chosen life, without fear of being disappointed, since the Spirit has been poured into our hearts. In prayer we continually express faith, hope, and love.

Prayer must also reach out to others and embrace the world. It may be personal, but it can never be privatistic. In prayer we remember the past, especially what God accomplished in Jesus Christ. We celebrate the present, and we reach out for the future. Eucharist prayer sustains a community's oneness in the Lord.

In prayer we long for the time when the Lord will return in triumph. Individual believers and faith communities will be united with him. The new age will dawn in its fullness, and salvation will be complete. We anticipate his coming by asking to know now the power of his resurrection (Phil 3:14). We gaze toward heaven, as we wait in prayer for his coming.

Paul views prayer as growing more aware that we are children of the Father in Jesus Christ the Son and that as such we are to live by the Spirit. In this life God calls us to a deep familiarity through mutual knowledge and love that will end with our being united to God in Christ. We are less than "natural" children, because Christ is God's only Son. But we are more than "adopted" children, that is, children by a legal action, because through baptism we have become one with God's Son. At present the Spirit enables us to address God as "Abba! Father!" In the end all creation will submit to God and all believers will be one with the God and Father of our Lord Jesus Christ.

Paul's view of prayer can inform how we pray. It suggests that we address our prayer to God as our Father, center it in Jesus Christ, and depend on the Spirit who empowers us to pray in our weakness. We might see our prayer as expressing the faith that we have received God's love as a gift, the hope that enables us to choose life without fear, and the love that responds to God's love. In prayer we can reach out to include others and embrace the world. We can express our deepest desire for God, a desire that will be partially fulfilled in this life, but will be satisfied only when we are united with God in Jesus Christ.

Forms of Prayer

Selecting passages in Paul's letters that appear to be prayers can be difficult. For Paul wrote letters to communicate with different communities, not to communicate with God. In this sense there are no prayers in the letters. But still Paul often reports on his prayer for the communities, and he includes several different prayer forms.

The prayer forms reflect his Jewish background. Above all they show how he succeeded in communicating a deep spirit of prayer to the communities he addressed. The prayers in his letters also disclose the character, content, and orientation of his continual communication with God.

Paul greets each community with the same basic formula: "Grace and peace be yours from God our Father and the Lord Jesus Christ" (2 Thes 1:2). Sometimes Paul expands the formula with words or phrases about God the Father and Jesus Christ. The solemnity of this greeting suggests that Paul may have adapted it from a popular formula used in the Christian liturgy. With it he sends his readers the grace and peace available to them through Jesus Christ their Lord. This form may also echo an ancient priestly blessing: "The Lord bless you and keep you. The Lord make his face to shine upon you, and be gracious to you. The Lord lift up his countenance upon you and give you peace" (Num 6:24-26).

Paul may well have created the formal thanksgiving with which he begins each letter. He first gives thanks and then makes a request: "I thank my God always when I remember you in my prayers, because I hear of your love and of the faith which you have toward the Lord Jesus and all the saints, and I pray that the sharing of your faith may promote the knowledge of all the good that is ours in Christ" (Phlm 4-6). The movement from thanksgiving to petition reflects the Christians' situation. For they are both grateful that the new age has already begun and aware of their needs until it has been fully established. When Paul prays for each community, he makes his prayer with profound joy and gratitude for what they have already received.

Spontaneous prayers occur throughout Paul's letters. Some, such as the following, resemble the traditional Jewish benediction: "Blessed be the God and Father of our Lord Jesus Christ, the Father of mercies and God of all comfort, who comforts us in all our affliction, so that we may be able to comfort those who are in any affliction, with the comfort with which we ourselves are comforted by God" (2 Cor 1:3-4). For the Jewish people the benediction was the central form of prayer, the prayer of the great festivals like Passover. Paul uses the benediction form less often than his thanksgiving form. In both forms, however, he witnesses before God that his gift in Christ has been received with gratitude.

Paul includes doxologies in his letters. In them he praises God's glory and power, majesty and splendor, and especially God's action in Jesus Christ: "To the only wise God be glory for evermore through Jesus Christ! Amen" (Rom 16:27). Doxologies occur throughout the Hebrew Scriptures and were central to Jewish public worship. Paul found this form well suited to letters, which would be read at the community's public worship.

In Galatians Paul incorporates a doxology into the initial greeting: "Grace to you and peace from God the Father and our Lord Jesus Christ, who gave himself for our sins to deliver us from the present evil age, according to the will of our God and Father, to whom be the glory for ever and ever. Amen" (Gal 1:3-5). In Romans he begins and ends his discussion of salvation for Jews and Gentiles with an outburst of praise: "God who is over all be blessed for ever. Amen" (Rom 9:5). "For from him and through him and to him are all things. To him be glory for ever. Amen" (Rom 11:36).

With brief, spontaneous prayers Paul maintains a climate of praise and gratitude throughout his letters: "But thanks be to God, who gives us the victory through our Lord Jesus Christ" (1 Cor 15:57). "But thanks be to God, who in Christ always leads us in triumph, and through us spreads the fragrance of the knowledge of him everywhere" (2 Cor 2:14). "Thanks be to God for his inexpressible gift!" (2 Cor 9:15). Paul addressed his thanks to God, and he often referred to Jesus Christ in whom God acted to save the world. With these unexpected prayers sprinkled throughout his letters, Paul sustains the tone of gratitude and praise that he announced in the initial greeting and thanksgiving.

Prayers also express Paul's wishes, hopes, and dreams for the communities to whom he writes. He commends them to God: "May the God of hope fill you with all joy and peace in believing, so that by the power of the Holy Spirit you may abound in hope" (Rom 15:13). This form occurs at the beginning, in the body, or at the end of a letter. Paul prays to God or to Jesus or to both for whatever the community needs to keep them growing in faith and witnessing to others: "Now may our God and Father himself, and our Lord Jesus, direct our way to you; and may the Lord make you increase and abound in love to one another and to all men, as we do to you, so that he may establish your hearts unblamable in holiness before our God and Father, at the coming of our Lord Jesus with all his saints" (1 Thes 3:11-13).

Paul ends all his letters except Romans with a solemn benediction that echoes the initial greeting. It envelops the letter in formal prayer: "Grace to you and peace" (1 Thes 1:1). "The grace of our Lord Jesus Christ be with you" (1 Thes 5:28). Again Paul prays that the community continue to develop and grow in the Lord through constantly remaining open to receive his grace and his peace: "Grace to you and peace from God our Father and the Lord Jesus Christ" (2 Cor 1:2). "The grace of the Lord Jesus Christ and the love of God and the fellowship of the Holy Spirit be with you all" (2 Cor 13:14).

These different forms attest that Paul considered prayer essential to his ministry and to the life of the communities he founded. In solemn greetings and final blessings he sent them the grace and peace that was theirs in Jesus Christ. In formal thanksgivings and occasional benedictions he gave thanks for all that God had done and was doing in their lives, and he prayed for their current needs. In doxologies he praised God for the glory and power that had been revealed in Jesus Christ. Paul sustained that attitude of praise and thanks in brief spontaneous prayers. Finally, Paul expressed in prayer his wishes, hopes, and dreams for the communities in their struggles to grow in the Lord.

With these prayers Paul constantly turns to God in Christ. He reveals how his apostolic work was informed by prayer and how his letters can be regarded as the product of his prayer. We can make Paul's prayers our own by using them for individual prayer or in our common prayer as communities of faith.

Once again here are some questions for your reflection:

■ Is God calling you to prayer?
■ How would being a woman or man of prayer change you?
■ What does Paul teach you about prayer?
■ In what ways could you use Paul's prayers?
■ Is prayer related to accepting God's gift of love in Jesus Christ? If so, how? If not, why not?

9

Cases and Methods

Concrete cases of persons praying with Paul's letters and methods appropriate to such prayer can help us approach the letters with confidence that through them we may encounter God and God may encounter us in love. We now want to look at cases and methods for praying the prayers in Paul's letters, for praying out of our experience and in dialogue with Paul's experience, and for praying with Paul's message. I invite you to find yourself in the cases or to make whatever adjustments might be needed to bring them closer to your experience. The methods show you how to be with the letters and enter into them, so that praying with Paul's letters might enrich your life with God.

Praying Paul's Prayers

Praying prayers is sometimes considered merely a matter of reciting the words. But repeating the words and phrases of a prayer from different perspectives may better prepare us to encounter God than approaching God with our minds or imaginations. Here is an approach to praying with Paul's prayers.

■ Quiet down, so as to become more aware of God in whose presence you are. Take time to remember that you are with God. Let that work of your memory center and focus you on God.
■ Select one of Paul's prayers to which you are drawn. Read through it quietly and notice the person to whom the prayer is addressed, the person to whom you'll be saying these words. Quietly let yourself be present to that person and let that person be present to you. Ask for what you need: "I want to speak these words to you. I want them to be more than words."
■ Recite the words with the desire that they may say what you want to say, that they may carry whatever thoughts and feelings you want to share with God. Give whatever attention you have. Some days your

121

mindfulness may be total and complete and the words may say exactly what you want to say. At other times you may be unable to quiet the noise in your pressured world. You may find yourself fighting with the same words. Give whatever attention you have at the moment. Avoid the strained effort to control that often stifles prayer. Make the genuine effort to pray out of your life at the moment, whether focused or scattered.

■ Recite the prayer from start to finish. Direct it to God, savoring, insofar as you are able, the meaning of each word as you recite it. Rather than try to control the movement, let the prayer carry you along with its rhythm. One advantage in this method is that you can float along with the prayer and ride with its cadence.

■ When you have gone through the prayer, you may be drawn to recite it over and over again, like children who need to repeat the same thing several times to their parents.

■ You may want to choose the word or phrase that most appeals to you, the one that comes most easily to you, your favorite word, phrase, or line. Repeat it again and again. Relax with it. Let it meet you. Relish it. Let it nourish you. Let it lead you, as you want to pray. Stay with it as long as it feeds you. Then move on to another word and phrase.

■ You may want to choose the word or phrase that carries difficulty for you. Let it replay itself in you again and again and notice what you feel, what happens to you when you recite it, what it may say to you about yourself or about your dealings with God. Let the words and your difficulty with them melt, as it were, carrying you to God with whom there is no difficulty you cannot discuss. At other times you may want to rest with the meaning of each word in the prayer. Say the first word and continue meditating on that one word as long as you find meaning and consolation. If you find in one or two words abundant matter for your thoughts and feelings, don't be anxious to move on.

■ Most important, let God into your prayer, meet him, and pray spontaneously about whatever surfaces. When that happens, let yourself encounter God in love. Return to the formal prayer when more spontaneous dialogue has ended. For you are praying Paul's prayers precisely because you desire to deepen your personal relationship with God.

We might find this method particularly useful when Paul's prayer articulates thoughts and feelings that we are unable to express in our own words. When we are grateful for friends and loved ones, we might bring them to mind and move to one of Paul's thanksgiving prayers (Phil 1:3-11). When we are deeply struck by the action of God in the world, we might let one of Paul's benedictions express our praise and wonder (2 Cor 9:5). When we experience deep inner movement but don't know what it is, we might pray one of Paul's hymns (Rom 16:27). When we are unable to speak because of our weakness, we might let ourselves be carried by Paul's prayer that his thorn in the flesh be removed (2 Cor 12:7-9). As we repeat Paul's words, they begin saying themselves in us and gradually become our words to God.

As we move along in the ways of prayer, we might want to carry a small stock of our favorite prayers, including some of Paul's, that we can fall back on in time of need. Because they are ready-made formulas, they may at first seem impersonal. But as we repeat them, as we break them in like a new pair of shoes, they sink deeper into our mind and heart. The prayers begin to shape us, as we find in them a distinctive, personal meaning. No wonder that the great spiritual teachers found this method particularly well suited to prepare a person to encounter God. Men and women who used this method were often led to higher forms of contemplation.

Dialoguing with Paul in Prayer

In Part I of this book we dialogued with Paul as diaspora Jew and Pharisee of the Pharisees, in his experience of the risen Lord, as missionary to the Gentiles and community organizer, and as a letter writer. We suggested how his experience might inform our lives. Now we want to hear the story of how a woman called Mary Ann dialogued with Paul in prayer. Then we will reflect on this method for use in our own prayer.

Mary Ann was a young sister in her mid to late twenties. After seven years in religious life she had to decide whether or not to request final vows, that is, to make a permanent commitment to her community. She belonged to a teaching community. Well liked and respected, she had been elected to the chapter of renewal and to the committee that was mandated to rewrite their constitutions. She was the youngest person elected. She enjoyed deepening her knowledge and appreciation of the charism that informed her congregation and loved the challenge of reflecting on how that charism might be lived out in today's world.

Mary Ann was always a bright, enthusiastic, idealistic sort of person. From her earliest days she had been drawn to the ideals in religious life, especially to living with other women in community and teaching in their schools. After making first vows, Mary Ann moved into one of the first small communities in her congregation. Six women close to her in age lived together in an apartment building and taught in the same girls' high school. Mary Ann had not taught before, but the other women supported and affirmed her initial efforts. They shared their experience with her and enabled her to quickly discover her strong gifts for teaching.

They also encouraged her to invite guests to their apartment, which made keeping in touch with friends outside school and community easy.

Mary Ann loved her craft and honing her skills as a teacher. She delighted in seeing her students win awards and scholarships. They sought her help in dealing with the normal issues in their teenage lives. She very quickly achieved success in both school and community and was well liked and popular.

As the young women approached final vows, Mary Ann's congregation asked them to live in a larger, more formal community. So Mary Ann moved from the apartment with the six other nuns and joined twenty-six women of different ages who lived together in a school convent. All had been teachers or administrators in large schools for girls. Some were still active, many semi-retired. Most were middle-aged women with life experiences, talents, and dreams that differed from Mary Ann's. She was the youngest member of this group by several years.

Mary Ann continued to teach with the same enthusiasm and success. But in the more structured community she met another reality in religious life: not everyone was perfect, not everyone embodied the ideals of the congregation. Pettiness and gossip were not uncommon in their conversation and seemed to contradict those ideals. People were nice to her, but life wasn't the same. These women didn't ask every day how her classes had gone. Nor was she any longer the focus of everyone's attention. She hardly knew the women she lived with.

Religious life stopped being ideal, and Mary Ann grew disillusioned. Horrified by the gossip and bitter complaining, she felt that religious life was a farce. She resented suggestions that she was too involved with her students. After a time she realized that she could also gossip and complain with the best of them. While reflecting on her two experiences of community, she was struck by the contrast between them.

As she thought about final vows, Mary Ann named three pieces that came together in her young religious life: the idealism of her formation years, her amazing success with the girls in school, the different living situations. She had worked hard at being a good nun and a good teacher. People had lined up at her door in both cases to tell her that she was a success. But coming to final vows raised questions: Can I live this life? Do I want to? What does this life entail? As she began to review her situation, she reflected on rewriting the constitutions, on the work of teaching, and on the women she had lived with. Nothing was clear.

The school year left Mary Ann exhausted. She had spent long hours with the girls, felt attacked and criticized by the nuns who told her she was getting too involved, and was confused by popularity issues. Emotionally strung out, she had no idea what the nuns meant about her being too entangled with the students. For the first time she was criticized rather than supported. She felt trapped and admitted to another nun: "What else could I have done? The girls were in trouble and needed someone to listen to them. I couldn't help it if they lined up at my door." Mary Ann described the predictable hazards of a young, idealistic teacher in her first fervor, a vivacious woman whom teenage girls were bound to admire.

Mary Ann intended to write her letter about final vows during the directed retreat immediately after the school year and before beginning work with the committee rewriting the constitutions. She was not in the best of spirits. She was fed up with her community. In her mind they were nothing more than bitter old ladies about whom little good could be said. After school ended on Wednesday, she exhausted herself getting grades to the office by the Friday night deadline. After that she tidied up her classroom, went to the graduation celebration, and chaperoned the dance.

Sunday morning she packed a suitcase and dragged her body to Mass in the convent chapel. The second reading was from Philippians 3. In the homily the priest explained the passage, dwelling at length on Paul's great love for God, on what a great missionary he was, and on how he gave up everything because Jesus Christ was the center of his life. Mary Ann hated the homily. In her fatigue she felt dissatisfied with everyone and everything, including herself.

That afternoon she arrived at the retreat house. Her director suggested that she needed rest and that she should not write the letter about final vows until the need rose in her. Her director further suggested that Mary Ann let God's Son/sun shine on her, that she let herself feel what that Son/sun was like on her skin, take a nap whenever she got tired, and be sure to eat dinner. Her director's final suggestion was that Mary Ann might try looking at a text from Scripture. The best text would be any that might be running around inside her. She should simply be with the text without working. She needed to trust God enough to rest in him, since that's what she would be doing for all eternity.

Feeling daring, Mary Ann went outside in short shorts and a sleeveless blouse. She lay down on a towel in the sun. Sometime later, because it was the right way to make a retreat, she went to the chapel to pray. Her attention soon wandered to the text from Paul that she had heard at Mass that morning. She mused about it and let it amble around inside her. Her mind roamed to her awful year in community, to how tired she was, and to what a bad homily she had heard. But the year had gone wonderfully well in school. The girls had learned so much, and she had gotten such a joy out of teaching them. She had done a good job and could taste her success. She had honed her skills. She would continue to improve at the teaching she most loved. She filled up with a heady satisfaction.

Mary Ann next thought about the girls—all-American girls from middle-class families: daughters of fireman, successful factory workers, and post office employees. But how awful life was for many of them, how much pain they carried around inside them without the other girls ever knowing. Some continually faced difficult scenes at home with their families. One's parents were getting divorced, another's father had died, another's brother was on drugs. One girl left school because she was pregnant.

Mary Ann's thoughts wandered to what she would do about final vows. She recalled all that the charism and ideals of her congregation meant to her. What she had learned and heard for the past seven years deeply inspired her, as did the ideal of what living the vows could and should mean. She thought about how hard it had been to combine good community life with being as present to the girls in schools as she wanted to be. The days just weren't long enough to be a good religious and also a good teacher.

Suddenly a sickening fear and sadness arose in Mary Ann. She felt inadequate: "I can't do it. It's so ideal. I am moved to tears by its beauty, the call to mission, and the support of community. I can be an excellent teacher. I love the work. I love the girls. But the ideals of community are beyond my reach. I can't live the vows." She felt overwhelmed.

Her intense feelings played against what she had experienced at Mass that morning. She picked up Philippians 3 and read through the passage. She heard not so much the text as the priest saying that we can become like Paul if we let Jesus Christ become the center of our lives, if we want nothing but God. It was too much for Mary Ann: "I can't do that. That was fine for Paul. But he had a horse and got knocked off it. I've never even been on a horse." Mary Ann started to cry and shut the Bible. She just wanted to see the retreat director, call to tell her superior she was leaving religious life, pack her suitcase, and look for a job with the American Can Company. She cried for a very long time, as though deep inner wells of tears would never run dry.

To distract herself from her tears, she reread the text from Paul. She moved her lips but did not read out loud, since she was in the chapel. She began to dialogue with Paul about the line that kept replaying itself in her: "For his sake I have suffered the loss of all things, and count them as refuse, in order that I may gain Christ" (3:8). She said: "I can't do this." But then the words changed. She began to hear them as spoken to her in the intensely emotional context of her retreat. She kept hearing the same phrase, but also the priest's exhortation that she should do what Paul had done.

Mary Ann thought of all that she would have to give up, all that was so important to her: Would she have to give up contact with her parents and family? What if she weren't allowed to teach? What if the community asked her to be an administrator? As she grew more fearful and discouraged, she became more convinced that she could not live the ideals of religious life. It might be meant for others. It was clearly not meant for her.

Without knowing she was doing so, she began telling Paul that she couldn't make Christ the center of her life: "That's fine for you. You were on a horse and got kicked off. The risen Lord was right there, and others led you to Damascus. Ananias was there to tell you what God wanted of you, and the community welcomed you with open arms. All I have in my community are old biddies. You joined a loving community. Even though you had killed their brothers and sisters, they welcomed you and took care of you. All my community does is tell me that I overextend myself and get too involved with the students. What's wrong with what I'm doing? I can't possibly do what you did." Mary Ann continued dialoguing with Paul until her confused tale was played out in her.

Mary Ann then heard from inside her: "You're not listening to what I'm saying. You're listening to what the priest said in his homily but not to what I want to say to you."

Mary Ann went back to Paul's text and read: "If any other persons think they have reason for confidence in the flesh, I have more ..." (3:4).

She talked to Paul: "That's it, Paul. You're qualified, and I'm not. I'm a good teacher, but they may make me an administrator or something else. Everyone says that I get too involved with the girls and that superiors had better look into this before approving me for final vows."

Paul said, "Read the words. Read what I wrote."

Mary Ann read about his achievements: "as to the law a Pharisee, as to zeal for religion a persecutor of the Church, as to righteousness under the law blameless" (3:5-6). She asked: "Was all that true?"

Paul answered: "Yes, I did it well and with the strong conviction that I was right. It was not easy, but it was immensely satisfying. I knew what I had to do, and I did it. I gave it my very best shot. I was a good Pharisee. I worked hard for my religion in persecuting the Church."

When Paul said "religion," Mary Ann reacted. She had entered religious life. In that life she had felt much more persecuted than persecuting. But she had gossiped along with the others. She had complained with the best of them. That realization startled her and broke through the feelings that were recycling themselves within her. She asked: "Paul, what made the difference?"

She read again: "For his sake I suffer the loss of all things, and count them as refuse, in order that I may gain Christ and be found in him" (3:8). All of a sudden Paul's words broke into the weight of discouragement that was oppressing her, almost as the sun breaks through storm clouds.

Mary Ann said: "That's what I want too. I want to gain Christ and be found in him." She moved in a dialogue that was sometimes with Paul, sometimes with Christ. Sometimes she wasn't sure with whom. She just kept saying, "That's what I want." She let her heart move until the dialogue became a wordless longing: "That is really what I want. Nothing else matters." Even the little old ladies in the convent began to look different. Another five years in that community became more than bearable. With that Mary Ann went to bed.

Next morning she felt ready to begin her retreat. Her director pointed out that she had already begun. She should move with the prayer inside her, go back to Paul, and stay with whatever moved and drew her mind and heart. If she got frightened, she would ask Paul if he had ever been frightened. Her director said: "Don't try to get rid of the fear. Speak out of it. Tell Paul that last night all you wanted was Christ, but that now you are really scared about what that might mean."

Mary Ann returned to the same line: "... that I may gain Christ and be found in him." As she talked about that with Paul, she again realized that this was what she really wanted. Gaining Christ and being found in him provided no pat answers and yet answered every question fundamentally. She had no decision to make about final vows, only decisions about when she would write the letter asking for them.

In the late afternoon Mary Ann began feeling quite agitated again. In her room she went back to the text and read it out loud, as though Paul were present and saying the words to her. As she read about Paul's achievements, her fears returned. She said to Paul, "I want what you wanted. But I can't do it. You had this wonderful experience of the risen Lord. But I haven't." She kept repeating these words over and over again.

Paul then said to Mary Ann, "I am no longer striving for perfection by my own efforts."

She responded, "You mean I don't need to do it myself."

"No. All you have to do is want to gain Christ. God will do the rest. I haven't become perfect yet, and neither have you. What's important is to keep wanting the perfection that comes from faith in Jesus Christ."

That much seemed possible to Mary Ann. She might have to go without guarantees that she would live the religious life well. But she could keep running to capture the prize. All she had to do was keep remembering that finding Christ and being found in him would make sense of her life. Paul's words carried more than meaning, but she didn't know what. She only knew that the expression was important to her.

Reflections

Mary Ann dialogued with Paul. In and through that dialogue she touched her desire to know Jesus Christ. She wanted him to be the center of her life. Dialoguing with Paul was a turning point in her religious awareness, and the text has remained a touchstone to which she often returns when she gets caught in old fears and disillusionment. She lives out of and is nourished by the memory of its truth.

Other experiences in Paul's life besides that encountered by Mary Ann might also lend themselves to this style of prayer. One experience is Paul's early life in Tarsus when he grew more convinced of his Jewish heritage while remaining open to the Hellenistic culture around him. We may be challenged to deepen our Christian faith and live according to its values in a dominant, secular culture. A second experience of Paul's was his encounter with the risen Lord when God invited him to swim less and float more, to drive less and take more buses (Gal 1:11-17). Paul began to let himself be carried by a power other than his own, by Jesus Christ crucified and risen. God may challenge us in our adulthood to float more and take more buses, to live less out of personal achievements and with more gratitude for the gift of his love.

A third experience that might help us dialogue with Paul in prayer is his plea to be delivered from the thorn in the flesh when he learned how physical weakness could ground him more firmly in God (2 Cor 12:7-10). His sufferings revealed how he was incorporated into the dying and rising of Christ. We can come to the same recognition about the meaning of our sufferings. Dialoguing with Paul in prayer will help us articulate our experience and discover in it an invitation to deepen our relationship to God. Here is a method you might find helpful.

■ Become aware of God in whose presence you are as you pray.
■ Stand in your own experience and begin to let Paul tell you about his experience. For example: "We are afflicted in every way, but not crushed; perplexed, but not driven to despair; persecuted, but not forsaken; struck down but not destroyed" (2 Cor 4:8-9). Let Paul speak, so that you might listen.
■ Out of your experience begin to dialogue with Paul. As your mind and heart are moved in this conversation, attend to the resemblances and differences that emerge and notice how Paul might influence your life.

■ Listen also for God who may want to communicate with you in and through the dialogue with Paul. Gradually let yourself move from interacting with Paul to communicating with God in prayer.

Praying with Paul's Message

In Part II of this book we worked to find meaning in Paul's message. We studied what that message meant to Paul and his communities, and we reflected on what it might mean to us today. We presented the drama of God's action in Jesus Christ in three scenes: dying and rising in Christ, God's plan for the world, and individuals and communities in the new age. Now we want to tell the story of Tom. When he prays passages from Paul's letters, he is drawn to particular statements about God's love and forgiveness. Through the statements he moves into the symbol of God as his Father. We will suggest methods by which we might move from finding meaning in Paul's message to encountering God in prayer.

Tom was raised in a traditional Lutheran family with strong ethnic roots. As a child and early teenager, he attended worship services each Sunday with his family. He also participated in the other activities at church. In college, however, he began to question his religion. Lutherans talked a great deal about God, but God seemed to make little difference in their lives. Moreover, God seemed to have nothing to do with his own life. Soon after college Tom married in the church. Without knowing why, he had his children baptized. But God continued to seem distant from his everyday life experience. Gradually he drifted away from church-going.

After eight years together, Tom and his wife divorced. This was precipitated by her having an affair with another man. Tom was deeply angry at his wife, at the church, at life. But instead of facing his anger he had an affair. When he thought of God at all, he practically denied that he existed. He was so unaware of his anger that he never stopped to reflect on why he needed to deny it. Nor did he work through his explosive bitterness.

As Tom explored being single, he gradually came to like the freedom it brought him. Visiting privileges enabled him to stay close to his sons who lived a few blocks away with their mother and her second husband. Professionally, he moved from public health work to the private world of business. He rose quickly in his company and began building within it his own empire. A highly competitive man, Tom usually succeeded in what he set out to accomplish.

For a while Tom dated several women, and then he met someone whom he grew to care for. As he imagined their getting married, however,

Tom began to realize that he could no longer run from anger about his first marriage. He knew that his former wife had been unfaithful, but he had also failed in their marriage. As he grew more serious about the woman he was dating, he grew more afraid that he might not succeed in a second marriage.

At this time his first wife moved to the west coast, because her second husband had been transferred. Distance now separated Tom from his sons. Remaining a father to them had been easy when they lived six blocks away from each other. He had taken their relationship for granted. But what would being their father mean with them in California? Tom felt strongly that he was losing what was most precious in his life—his role as father to his children. Tom visited his sons as often as possible. Either they came to the midwest for short visits, or he went to the west coast. Distance forced Tom to focus on what lies at the heart of being their father. He wanted to make the best use of their time together. If he hadn't been a good husband to his first wife, he at least wanted to be the best father he could to his children.

Tom's failure in marriage and his wrenching separation from his sons seemed to till his inner soil. Tillers break up what is hard in the ground, but they also cut and make furrows. Tom grew more open to the pain of how much he needed and wanted to be a good father to his children. Opportunities seemed to be dying.

Tom sought help in counseling. He was in love and wanted to marry. But he couldn't survive a second failure. The first had cost everyone too much pain. In counseling he touched the deep feelings that he had ignored. A chasm separated those feelings from his ability to communicate them to himself and others. Counseling helped him begin to bridge that distance. A new sense of himself gradually came to birth.

Tom married the woman he loved. After a time of initial happiness they began to sense that something was missing from their lives. When they looked for what this might be, they found that church might fill their emptiness. So they joined a church where they could hear a good sermon, belong to a welcoming community, and take part in service activities. At the same time their love for each other contributed to Tom's wife having a profound religious conversion. It left her wanting to learn more about prayer.

Tom joined his wife in seeking advice about prayer. He knew that something was still missing in his life, that there had to be more to his life than he had found. If he were ever to be a whole person, he must be reconciled to his divorce. Filled with anger, Tom continued to feel that he had been a failure. He also knew that he wanted to be a good father to his sons and a good husband to his second wife. He would also like God to draw closer to his life. But at this time God seemed nothing more than a harsh judge who stood outside Tom.

As Tom prayed, he wondered whether God might love him, whether God might be a center for him in his life. That wonder led him to see that he must face the well of bad feelings around his first marriage, deal with the issue of forgiveness in his life, and put that marriage to rest. Whenever he had competed in the past whether in business or in sports, he always won. But he had failed in marriage. So Tom asked himself: Is God so loving as to forgive me? What is forgiveness? How can I forgive if God doesn't forgive?

Tom started to pray with Paul, specifically with the fifth and eighth chapters of Romans. As he read and reread these chapters, Tom was struck by the statements: "For God has done what the law, weakened by the flesh, could not do: sending his own Son in the likeness of sinful flesh he redeemed sin in the flesh.... God shows his love for us in that while we were yet sinners Christ died for us.... We also rejoice in God through our Lord Jesus Christ, through whom we have now received our reconciliation" (Rom 5:3, 8, 11).

When Tom met this text about a forgiving, loving, reconciling God, he talked to it, chewed on it, even fought with it. But he found no meaning in it. He wanted to forget about it, but the text almost haunted him. He kept coming back to it in spite of himself. As he continued to wrestle, he realized that he could not recall an experience of forgiving or being forgiven. He had known in his head that God was loving, but his heart had not been convinced. God began, however, to move near enough for Tom to spend three months telling him that he didn't know how to forgive.

Tom and his wife planned to take a vacation with his sons on the west coast. His eldest son was in junior high. He was not a bad boy, but he was experiencing normal growing pains—being antagonistic to everything, refusing to study, and mouthing off in school. One day he stole something. With a couple of friends he went to a drug store, took a razor, some blades, and some candy bars, and got caught. The owner called his mother to the store and confronted her with what her son had done. She was angry; her son was terrified. Later she told him: "Just wait until your father gets here. You're going to change your ways. You're going to stop picking on your brother. You're going to start working in school."

When Tom walked into the house, the first thing he heard about was his son's shoplifting. He exploded with anger. When the dust settled, his son asked: "Are we still going on vacation? Do I have to stay home while my brother goes? Are you ashamed of me? Do you still want to be my father?"

His father answered: "It never occurred to me to be ashamed. Of course I still want to be your father. And you're going with us on vacation. But first you and I are going to have a little talk. Then we're going to walk back to the store. You're going to pay the owner for what you stole, and then you're going to ask him what you can do to make up for what you've done. You're going to do something for the man. Then you're going to mow someone's lawn or clean out someone's garage to make enough money to reimburse me. When you've finished the chores, we'll go on vacation."

His son asked: "Will I get to do all the things we planned?"

"Of course you will. But first you have to do the things I've said."

"Well, why?"

"Because this is what happens when you do something wrong. These are the consequences. This man has every right to be angry at you. He could have turned you in to the police. He was very nice to you. Now you have to do something for him."

His son spent the afternoon assembling heavy cardboard boxes at the drug store. When he got home, his father told him to shower and get dressed to go out to dinner. His son asked: "Do you still want me to come?" Tom reassured him that he did. At dinner Tom noticed that his son was unusually quiet. He asked over and over: "Are you sure that I get to go on vacation, and not just my brother?" His father kept saying, "Yes, of course." The son was content for the rest of the evening.

On vacation Tom took a long tramp with his son in the woods. He wanted to talk over what had happened. After little or no conversation, his son said to Tom: "Are you mad at me?"

"No, I'm not mad at you."

"Are you still proud to call me your son?"

"Well, of course I am. What made you think that I might not be proud of you? I was very angry at what you did. And I don't ever want to hear that you did it again. You were very wrong. I made you work to teach you that you must pay for your actions. You stole, and you paid the consequences. But nothing could ever make me stop loving you or wanting you to be my son."

Suddenly Tom remembered the text from Paul: "For all who are led by the Spirit of God are children of God.... When we cry 'Abba! Father!' it is the Spirit himself bearing witness with our spirit that we are children of God.... Nothing will be able to separate us from the love of God in Christ Jesus our Lord" (Rom 8:15, 18, 38). After this experience with his son, Tom began to live in these texts. Until this time forgiveness had been little more than a word, a surface reality, a pardoning of minor offenses. Now Tom began to know the depth of forgiveness—his own and God's.

Tom realized how God had given him the strong desire to be a good father to his son in trouble. Wasn't that what forgiveness was all about? He chose to be a father to his son, right at the point where his son had done something wrong. He may never have loved his son more than in what followed. Tom suddenly realized: "My God, if I feel this way about my son, how much more you must feel this way about me!"

The texts continued to push into his life, as Tom mused: "God must want to be a Father if he would send his Son." He began to live with the reality of God's love for him, as a Father's love for his child. He found himself able to approach the God who had seemed so distant. Now he could begin to relate to him as a forgiving Father and to see himself as forgivable.

He also began to accept the consequences of his divorce. It would always hurt, but Tom gradually grew in compassion for his sense of failure and his lack of forgiveness. He began to focus his energy on building a good life with those he loved. He no longer needed to carry the immense burden of anger and failure. Nothing, not even these powerful feelings, could separate him from the love of Christ or prevent him from being a more loving husband and father. He stopped looking at forgiveness and began looking at the forgiver.

A. Passages

In praying with Paul, Tom started with passages from the fifth and eighth chapters of Romans. He used a method which has been called "Sacred Reading" (*Lectio Divina*) in which he moved from asking questions about the text to more affective prayer. It is an excellent method for praying with Paul's letters, especially for praying indicative passages or passages that move from statements to exhortation. Here is one way to practice the method:

■ After preparing for prayer and putting yourself in God's presence, *read* the passage from Paul. In a slow, meditative reading, dwell on each element in the text. Read the passage several times, out loud if possible, until something draws you or repels you.

■ At that point, begin to *meditate,* that is, to reason about what has awakened in your mind and heart. Ask questions about what the passage might mean: What are the major divisions? What are the key words and phrases? What techniques convey its meaning—questions, antitheses, repetitions? What is the dominant theme? How does each element contribute to the theme? How does the thought move? What draws you? What do you resist? Let yourself speak with God or Christ about your responses and any feelings accompanying them.

■ As you think about the passage, you may begin to sense resemblances with your life experiences. Those resemblances may lead you into dialogue in *prayer* with God or with Jesus Christ. Speak spontaneously, or remain silent in God's presence. Close the Scripture, and open your heart to this encounter. Remain in prayer as long as you are not too distracted. When distractions make prayer difficult, read the passage again and move from reading to meditation and from meditation to prayer.

B. Statements

Gradually, Tom took time to assimilate those statements that carried most meaning for him, statements about God's love and forgiveness. A method for letting a statement from Paul take deeper root in us, as we accept its truth with our minds and engage it with our hearts, is to focus in prayer on a statement that carries meaning for us, a statement we either feel attracted to or want to resist. Such statements might be:

■ "Christ died for our sins ... and he was raised on the third day" (1 Cor 15:3-5).

■ "I have been crucified with Christ; it is no longer I who live, but Christ who lives in me" (Gal 2:20).

■ "All of us who have been baptized into Christ Jesus were baptized into his death" (Rom 6:3).

■ "In Christ there is neither Jew nor Greek, slave nor free, male nor female" (Gal 3:28).

■ After preparing for prayer simply say the words to yourself; form the words by moving your lips or by saying them aloud. Whichever way you choose, repetition is key. Simply repeating the words without trying to understand them enables you to receive them into your heart, to let them become part of the texture of your inner life. Like a seed, the statement begins to disintegrate and break open, so that its hidden truth might be revealed.

■ If the statement expresses a paradoxical truth—a metaphor—focus on the obvious contradiction in the terms. Let yourself be shocked, resist the statement, almost dismiss it as nonsense. Stay with the tension that the words create in you. Let it slowly disclose resemblances that were hidden. Let the literal meaning self-destruct and a deeper meaning begin to surface through the cracks.

■ As you savor the words you are repeating, as they blend with your life, you may find the sentences transformed to fit your experience, or you may focus attention on one part of the statement. After a while you may feel deeply nourished by the words. You may then feel drawn to speak spontaneously to God, or you may feel drawn to a loving silence. In any case, you listen attentively for the presence of God whom you wish to encounter in prayer.

C. Symbols

Finally, Tom was drawn into the symbol of "father," himself as father to his son who stole, God as Father to himself who failed in his first marriage. Praying with Paul's symbols—God as Father, the cross, the human body, an earthen vessel, and so on—means letting the symbols draw us into contact with the deeper reality that they can disclose. Symbols can mediate the transcendent power of God, and through them we can experience God's love and forgiveness. Different methods can help us pray with symbols. The following method has six steps.

■ As you enter into prayer, relax your body, empty your mind, and quiet your feelings. In Step 1, focus on the symbol as a reality outside yourself. For example, attend the individual parts of the cross at center stage—the height, the pieces of wood, the details of the body on the cross. Remain with this step, and with each of the following steps, as long as they hold your attention. In Step 2, attend to the feeling tone of the symbol. Is the cross warm or cold, hard or soft, appealing or repelling? In Step 3, be aware of how your feelings respond to the symbol. As you draw closer to the cross, are you more attracted than repelled, more comfortable with approaching it than worried about getting close? Do you want to turn away?

■ In Step 4, let yourself become the symbol. Enter into the cross and become absorbed into it until you are one with it and it is one with you. In Step 5, experience yourself and the symbol become one with the whole world. You and the cross expand to embrace all men and women, all creation, and you experience all creation as one with yourself in the cross. In Step 6, rediscover your identity within the oneness with all creation. Experience yourself as an individual in union with all creation and with the cross of Jesus Christ.

■ At any moment in this six-step prayer, the symbol may disclose to you the presence of Jesus Christ and the Father. When that happens, simply move through the symbol to encounter them, and remain with them as long as the prayer continues.

No one can predict the outcome of praying with Paul's letters. When we feel strongly and deeply connected to God and Jesus Christ, we will want to respond with Paul: "To the only wise God be glory for evermore through Jesus Christ! Amen!" (Rom 16:27). At other times we may feel a deep sense of inner peace, even when our lives seem chaotic, since we have learned from Paul that God's power sustains us in our weakness. When prayer seems a total waste of time, we might reflect with Paul that our relationship with God is not to be measured by how we feel but rather by how we participate in the mystery of God's love revealed in Christ's death and resurrection.

Epilogue:

Paul and Contemporary Wisdom about Adult Life

We have dialogued with Paul as diaspora Jew and Pharisee of the Pharisees, in his experience of the risen Lord, as missionary to the Gentiles and community organizer, and as letter writer. We have found meaning in Paul's message about dying and rising in Christ, about God's plan for the world, and about individuals and communities in the new age. We have explored what praying with Paul's letters means and described cases and methods for prayer. Now we want to suggest some resemblances between Paul's experience and message and contemporary authors who write about adult development—Erik Erikson, James W. Fowler, Daniel J. Levinson, Evelyn and James Whitehead.

These authors tell us stories about other men and women in their adult lives. As we move through different transitions and stages, their findings help us clarify our experience and provide wisdom about how to navigate the journey. Adult development is a gradual transformation in the direction of greater internal differentiation, increased ability to deal with complexity, and a stronger sense of personal stability. We are enabled to make meaning in an ever more complex world and thereby contribute more to society.

How can we talk about resemblances between Paul and contemporary gossip about adult life? Aren't we "psychologizing" Paul? Can we compare what Paul understood to be more outer, objective, historical realities with what psychology describes as more inner, subjective, psychic realities? We recognize that Paul was not a contemporary adult, that modern psychology was not available to him. But didn't he touch the same realities as modern authors? We want to avoid the dangers inherent in psychologizing Paul, in making him more inward-looking than he was. But from the vantage point of our more differentiated consciousness and our culture formed by psychology, we can see in Paul's letters connections with the process of adult development that he himself could not have seen. Without imposing our twentieth century awareness on Paul, we want to suggest ways in which he might dialogue with the contemporary wisdom about adult life.

Network of Relationships

Paul presents Christian individuals and communities as finding their identity in a network of relationships. Through faith and baptism they are incorporated into Christ's death and participate in his resurrection. In Christ they are children of God, and they drink of the Holy Spirit. Their radical equality destroys the barriers that normally separated Jew from Gentile, slave from master, man from woman. In community they are to maintain a healthy balance between unity and diversity, so that they might realize their potential as members of the body of Christ. At the Eucharist they share the same bread and drink from one cup to express their oneness in the same Lord. Empowered by the Spirit, they direct their prayer in Christ to "Abba! Father!" And they trace that Spirit's action in their lives.

Paul looks at how Christians relate to Christ and the Father and at how they are to relate to each other in community. He is not so interested in how they are to relate to the world outside. His letters are filled with practical advice on issues that arose in communities struggling for a sense of their identity in that complex world. But he was not concerned about changing its social, political, or economic structures. He was convinced that the world was about to end with the parousia. So he focused on life within the community.

In *Seasons of a Man's Life*, Daniel J. Levinson talks about the "individual life structure" as the pattern of relationships, roles, and consistent points of our exchange with the world. This life structure includes our love relationships, our family ties, and the friendship and acquaintance networks that sustain us. It includes our religious affiliations and involvements as well as our work and professional roles and societies. It includes the patterns of our leisure activities, our public life as citizens, and our private lives. It is made up of the ways we engage the world, on the one hand, and suffer the world's engagement with us, on the other. As we move from one season of our lives to another, this life structure undergoes development and modification. Though it would have taken time to bridge the huge distance between their cultures and language, I suggest that Levinson and Paul have similar understandings of how relationships contribute to human identity.

James W. Fowler, in his book *Becoming Adult; Becoming Christian*, discusses the community of faith formed around Jesus Christ. The community has found its identity in the impact of Christ's death and resurrection, and its energy originates in the powerful presence of his Spirit. The members of the community shape their identity around a shared story of cosmic significance. They participate in and identify with the central passion of that story. That passion forms their affections and guides their motivation. Virtues serve a community's central passion and move their affections to action. Though Paul would not understand Fowler's concepts and technical language, the two men are, I believe, touching the same reality.

Times of Transition

Paul drew on apocalyptic imagery to preach that the new age had already begun with the death and resurrection of Christ, but that it would not yet be fully established until his return. In the meantime, Christians live in the overlapping of the two ages. They are already saved from the powers of the old age, but not yet fully living in the grace of the new age. They live in a time of transition, a time of dying and rising with Christ, a time to struggle against the flesh and trace the Spirit.

In *Christian Life Patterns*, Evelyn and James Whitehead speak of adult transitions as the developmental challenges that can be expected to accompany a person's movement through adult life. We are challenged about how to be with others (intimacy), how to be creative and caring (generativity), and how to make sense of life (integrity). A transition is a crucial period of time in which we experience both increased vulnerability and heightened potential. As we begin to let go of a past that we have cherished, we feel discontinuous. We mourn the loss and move into ambiguity, as we wait for new meaning to unfold. We recruit persons and communities to support us with solidarity and compassion, so that we might fight the tendency to live in isolation.

In this overlapping time we look backward and forward. We look back to complete the work of the era that is ending, while we look forward to engage the tasks that call us into the new era. We live with ambiguity and confusion. Although we have already begun the new season, we have not yet put the old season to rest. I suggest that this "in-between" sense of time with its dying and rising resembles the eschatological tension that Paul considered essential to the Christian life.

Polarities in Tension

Paul often presents reality in terms of the tension between polarities. Polarities such as old age/new age, already/not yet disclose his both/and view of time. Others such as Adam/Christ, sin/grace, death/life, works/ faith, flesh/spirit, and despair/hope describe the either/or "fields of force" at work in God's plan for the world. Still others—weakness/power, folly/

wisdom—express the mystery and paradox of God's action in Christ. Paul also challenges the community to keep unity and diversity in a creative tension.

Erik H. Erikson sees the ages and phases of human life in terms of a sequence of emergent challenges and crises that a developing person must meet and that hold potential for new strength and virtue. Each crisis challenges the person to grow within the tension between polarities: trust and hope vs. mistrust, autonomy and will vs. shame, initiative and purpose vs. guilt, industry and competence vs. inferiority, identity and fidelity vs. confusion, intimacy and love vs. isolation, generativity and care vs. stagnation, integrity and wisdom vs. despair.

Maturing adults reap the fruits of having more or less successfully negotiated these crises. They have formed a strong foundation of basic trust and have grown into a healthy sense of independence. They take initiative, have a sense of purpose in their lives, and contribute productively to society. An adult sense of identity enables them to risk closeness to others. I suggest that Erikson can dialogue with Paul about adults who are creatively navigating the tension between basic human polarities.

In his book, *Stages of Faith,* James W. Fowler describes two adult stages of faith development. He reflects on how adults experience polarities. In the "individuative-reflective" stage adults gain a new awareness of polarities, as they can no longer avoid decisions about the tensions and ambiguities in life. They value individuality over group membership, subjectivity over objectivity, the power of their own feelings over critical reflection, self-fulfillment over care for others, and commitment to what is relative over struggling with an absolute reality.

As they live within these polarities, adults in this stage are more likely to dichotomize them into an either/or perspective than to hold them in creative tension. They might side with forces like grace and life that are in conflict with sin and death. They might ignore the fact that Paul sees Christians as living within the tension between those two opposed sets of forces.

Adults at the stage of "conjunctive faith" are more attuned to tensions that can cohere in a paradoxical balance: power in weakness, wisdom in foolishness, possibilities in pain, life in death. They no longer see life in either/or terms. More alive to the paradox in apparent contradictions, they tend to maintain opposites in creative tension. They hold together the tensions of being at the same time both old and young, masculine and feminine. They face their destructive and constructive tendencies, and they grow more aware of their conscious and shadow self. Truth has become more complex than most either/or categories can capture. It must be approached simultaneously from at least two or more perspectives. Paradox and apparent contradictions are intrinsic to truth. These adults would resonate with Paul's understanding and appreciation of the paradox in God's action in Christ.

Conversion or Self-Realization

Paul the Pharisee was in full charge of his life with God. The law was his way to God. He strove to observe it to perfection. Paul felt that by his works he was achieving and maintaining his right relationship with God. He was in control at all times. After he experienced the risen Lord, Paul recognized that all was gift and received that gift with faith. He had not deserved it, nor had he any control over it. In trust he accepted the gift and let it transform his life. He began to live by a power not his own, a power from God in Jesus Christ. He began to swim less and float more, to drive less and take more buses.

Paul later preached about God who revealed his love in the death and resurrection of Jesus Christ. He invited Jews and Gentiles, slaves and masters, men and women to receive that revelation as a pure gift and participate in it through faith and baptism. Those who accepted Paul's invitation formed communities that resembled the human body. They celebrated their differing gifts without losing a sense of their oneness in Christ. As they ate one bread and drank from one cup, they experienced deep compassion and strong solidarity with each other.

In *Becoming Adult: Becoming Christian,* James W. Fowler contrasts contemporary versions of destiny and self-actualization to the Christian vision of human vocation. Destiny and self-actualization lead to the assumption that we are or can be self-grounded persons who believe that we have within us and must generate from within us all the resources for creating a fulfilled and self-actualized life. In other words, we control our own destiny. In contrast, Fowler suggests that vocation is a call to partnership with God on behalf of the neighbor. Vocation constitutes a far more fruitful way to look at our specialness, our giftedness, our possibilities of excellence.

In a vocation perspective, personal fulfillment is part of communal fulfillment. We find ourselves by giving ourselves. In this perspective, self-actualization is not an end in itself but a by-product of fidelity to both our partnership with God and our action in serving God and the neighbor. Those who live in vocation cease competing with one another and turn to supporting each other. In vocation God calls us to celebrate and share our unique gifts with others for the common adventure. A Christian view of the human vocation suggests that partnership with the action of God may be the most fruitful principle for orchestrating our changing adult life structure. Once they found a common language,

I suspect that Paul and Fowler would find strong resemblances in their views of how persons and communities are to live in Christ.

According to the contemporary wisdom about adult life we can all expect at times to review the network of relationships in our lives, make judgments about it, and perhaps decide to change. We can expect to pass through important times of transition, struggle with polarities in tension, and meet life as profoundly paradoxical. We may also be called to cease struggling to realize our own destiny, so that we might enter into greater partnership with God. We have seen how Paul faced similar issues in his own time and culture and how his message enabled the members of his communities to grow as adult Christians. If this book has made Paul more accessible to us, as a companion in our adult lives, it will have served the purpose for which it was written.

Appendix:

Paul and Women

Was Paul the all-time male chauvinist or at heart a feminist? We might call him a chauvinist, since he seems to have told women to be subject to their husbands, to keep silent and not teach in liturgical assemblies, to dress modestly, and to work out their salvation through childbearing. Elsewhere, however, Paul sounds more like a feminist with the deep conviction that men and women are one in Christ, that the sexual differences between them must be respected, and that those differences do not mean that women are subordinate to men. Was Paul a chauvinist or a feminist? Perhaps he stands somewhere in between. Answers will emerge as we look at what Paul himself wrote and then at the tradition that bore his name, both the Gnostic fringe and the mainstream reaction.

Paul

Paul expressed his view that the sexes were equal in this passage: "For as many of you as were baptized into Christ have put on Christ. There is neither Jew nor Greek, there is neither slave nor free, there is neither male nor female; for you are all one in Christ Jesus" (Gal 3:27-28). He may have been quoting the formula that Christians were already using at baptism. He made it his own by including it in his letter. The formula proclaimed that through baptism Christian men and women were initiated into an inclusive community in which their oneness in Jesus Christ abolished the racial, social, or sexual inequalities that defined them in their society. Within the community, men and women were to live together as equals, no matter what their status outside the community. They might be powerless to change patterns of subordination in the Jewish and Hellenistic culture, but their life in community was to reflect the divine order in which God created male and female as equals (Gen 1). Men and women were to drop all cultural guises of subordination and model that order of created equality by the way they lived together in the Christian community.

145

Paul was not always consistent in carrying out his vision of racial, social, and sexual equality. As we have seen, he worked to abolish the inequalities between Jews and Greeks that stemmed from the law. To share his work, his travel, his meals, and his worship with Gentiles he violated his own training and background, his own convictions as a Pharisee. He challenged Peter for being inconsistent, he argued his case for equality before the leaders in Jerusalem, and he defended his Gospel against all attackers. For Paul was convinced that in Christ there is neither Jew nor Greek.

Paul affirmed the same equality for slaves and women, but he did not challenge the social structures that perpetuated their subordination. Because he regarded the present time as destined to end soon with the final in-breaking of the new age, Paul did not consider himself or his communities called to change the structures in society that oppressed slaves and women. Soon God would overturn those structures and establish the full equality anticipated by their baptism into Christ.

Nevertheless, Paul *does* maintain his view that men and women are equal when he discusses their roles in marriage (1 Cor 7:1-40). Some members in the community at Corinth had begun to claim that men should not have sexual intercourse with their wives, and they introduced an asceticism that threatened the values of marriage and human sexuality. Convinced that men and women were equal, Paul argued that they must also respect their sexual differences and honor sexuality in marriage.

In responding to the questions from Corinth, Paul almost always speaks explicitly to *both* men and women. Each enjoys the same freedom, and each carries the same responsibilities: "The husband should give to his wife her conjugal rights, and likewise the wife to her husband. For the wife does not rule over her own body, but the husband does; likewise the husband does not rule over his own body, but the wife does" (1 Cor 7:3-4). Furthermore, women and men are equally accountable in matters concerning temporary sexual abstinence, divorce and separation, mixed marriages and their dissolution, anxiety in and out of marriage.

Paul takes marriage or sexual relations within marriage for granted and demonstrates that the sexual differences between women and men in marriage do not contradict their radical equality. Above all, the differences do not suggest that wives must submit to their husbands.

Paul reflects the same tension between equality and differentiation in his discussion of dress at liturgical assemblies (1 Cor 11:2-16). In its present form this passage is one of Paul's most difficult compositions. He clearly demands that women cover their heads when they lead the community worship. Does he also imply that women are subordinate to men? Once again Paul takes for granted that both men and women lead the community in their liturgical assembly. For the Spirit has given gifts of prayer and prophecy without sexual discrimination. The problem at Corinth was not that women led the worship but that in doing so they dressed and appeared like men. At issue was not the equality of men and women in sharing liturgical leadership but their sexual differences. Women should be women, men should be men, and all should be able to recognize the men from the women.

Well-dressed women in Paul's day covered their hair with a cloth, however small. Without such a covering their hair was considered loose and untidy. Well-dressed men wore short hair and kept their heads uncovered. Paul urged women to wear their hair in the feminine style and men to wear their hair in the masculine style, so that the community might recognize the differences between them. He does not suggest that women are subordinate to men, but only that the differences between them should not be blurred.

The following verse from this passage is often quoted to prove Paul's chauvinism. In it Paul refers to the order in creation: "But I want you to understand that the head of every man is Christ, the head of a woman is her husband, and the head of Christ is God" (1 Cor 11:3). Here Paul might seem inconsistent in subordinating woman to man, man to Christ, and Christ to God in a strict, hierarchical line of authority. But the term "head" probably means "source" or "origin," rather than "lordship," and Paul seems to say that in creation every man's source is Christ, the source of woman is man (Gen 2), and the source of Christ is God. God created all other beings according to his divine order. Christ, the first-born, was involved with God in creation of man, and all three worked together to create woman. The order in creation establishes the differences between man and woman, but it does not affirm subordination.

With creation still in mind Paul later says: "For man was not made from woman, but woman from man. Neither was man created for woman, but woman for man" (1 Cor 11:8-9). Once again he seems to suggest that women are subordinate to men. But Paul balances that statement with another that stresses mutuality: "Nevertheless, in the Lord woman is not independent of man nor man of woman; for as woman was made for man, so man is now born of woman. And all things are from God" (1 Cor 11:11-12). Paul argues that men and women depend mutually on each other both in creation and in childbearing. The differences between them must remain obvious to all, even as they share equally the role of speaking God's word in prayer and prophecy to the assembled community.

Paul presumes the right of women to participate in his missionary work and in the activities of the communities he founded. His churches seemed to agree that women could lead as well as men. Women's names appear alongside those of men in a list of greetings (Rom 16:1-15). Paul singles out two women leaders who were at odds with each other, emphasizing that they have labored with him for the sake of the Gospel (Phil 4:2-3). He does not suggest that their participation differed from that of the men. Once again, Paul acts in accord with his conviction that in Christ there is neither male nor female.

However, once again Paul seems to contradict himself when he writes to the Corinthians: "As in all the churches of the saints, the women should keep silence in the churches. For they are not permitted to speak, but should be subordinate, as even the law says" (1 Cor 14:33-34). Several arguments converge to prove that Paul did not write these verses. First, they contradict Paul's discussion of dress in which he takes for granted that women lead the community's prayer and prophecy (1 Cor 11:2-16). Second, these verses interrupt the argument within this letter to the Corinthians that Paul is developing concerning prophetic activity. Without them his argument is clear and forceful. Third, Paul would hardly appeal to the law in support of his statement about women. Finally, these verses echo those written by authors in the later Pauline tradition (especially 1 Tim 2:11-12), who held that sexual differentiation meant that women be subordinate to men. A Pauline editor must have inserted these verses into the letter to the Corinthians as a marginal note to Paul's original letter. They were gradually incorporated into the text of the letter, so that Paul's authority might stand behind the subordination of women.

Gnostic Fringe

Gnostic tendencies began to emerge at Corinth in an exaggerated asceticism concerning sexual relations in marriage and in a tendency to abolish the different dress codes for men and women in the liturgy. We have seen how Paul responded to these situations. After his death, Christians, especially women, who continued to be attracted to these tendencies, formed a movement within the Pauline tradition. Since data is scarce, we must reconstruct the movement from apocryphal writings, from later Pauline (not Paul's) letters, and from patristic responses to later Gnostic sects.

At the root of the Gnostic tradition was an understanding of the resurrection that conflicted with Paul. According to Paul the resurrection of the Christian was in the future, when Christ would return in triumph. It would include the total person, both body and soul. Gentile Christians tended to find Paul's teaching difficult because in the resurrection, as they understood it, the soul would be released from the prison of the body, so that it might continue to live forever in freedom from matter.

In knowing Jesus Christ to be their Savior, these Christians believed that their real, spiritual self was already raised, that is, released from the body in which it had been imprisoned.

Consistent with how they viewed the resurrection, these Gnostic Christians considered themselves outside the order of creation. They tended to deny that which most characterizes the differences between the sexes, the marital act. Some prohibited marriage, and others opposed childbearing. Because they originated with the devil, marriage, intercourse, and procreation were evil (Saturnilus, circa 130 AD). Paul was thought to have taught this doctrine: "But he (Paul) deprives you men of wives and maidens of husbands, saying, 'Otherwise there is no resurrection for you, except you remain chaste and do not defile the flesh, but keep it pure'" *(Acts of Paul)*. According to these Gnostics, marriage was wrong, and those who marry should have no resurrection.

Mainstream

Against these Gnostic tendencies the mainstream within the Pauline tradition stressed that the sexes were different and that wives must submit to their husband to protect that difference. The order of creation included subordination in marriage. In fact, according to this tradition, the differences in the sexes could not be maintained without such subordination. Pauline authors (not Paul) adapted the patriarchal household codes that governed relationships between wives and husbands, parents and children, slaves and masters in the Jewish and Hellenistic culture. They urged women to submit to their husbands, remain silent in liturgical assemblies, and find their fulfillment in childbearing.

Household codes were common in late Judaism and in Hellenistic philosophy. Paul instructed his communities not to follow such codes but to live according to their radical equality in Christ. But later authors reintroduced them in his name to correct Gnostic exaggerations: "Wives, be subject to your husbands, as is fitting in the Lord. Husbands, love your wives, and do not be harsh with them" (Col 3:18-19). In adapting the code, however, this Pauline author stresses the mutual but not equal rights and obligations of wives and husbands. Wives are to submit to their husbands, but husbands are to love their wives. Within the proper subordination Christian love remains mutual and reciprocal. The husband's authority over his wife may be given in creation, but he must balance it with love and respect. For without mutual love wives submit with an empty obedience, and husbands exercise authority without any reference to Christ.

A later Pauline author finds resemblances between the subordination of wives to their husbands and that of the Church to Christ: "Be subject to one another out of reverence for Christ. Wives, be subject to your husbands, as to the Lord. For the husband is the head of the wife, as Christ is the head of the Church, his body, and is himself its Savior. As the Church is subject to Christ, so let wives also be subject in everything to their husbands. Husbands, love your wives, as Christ loved the Church and gave himself up for her that he might sanctify her.... Even so, husbands should love their wives as their own bodies" (Eph 5:21-26, 28).

Human institutions, such as the family, are meant to reflect the mystery of Christ's relationship to the Church. Again wives are to serve their husbands, and husbands are to love their wives. A wife's "subjection" means that she serves her husband and submits to his authority, and a husband's "love" means that he serves his wife and cares for her needs. For they are to model their mutual relationship on the union between Christ and the Church, a vital union of love and service. Marriage and the family provides the setting for actualizing the love of Christ in their love for each other, since their love resembles that of Christ who died to make the Church his bride.

By the time these later letters were composed not by Paul but by his followers, women no longer led the community in prayer in liturgical assemblies. They were told to dress modestly, participate in silence, and find their satisfaction in bearing children: "For Adam was formed first, then Eve; and Adam was not deceived, but the woman was deceived and became a transgressor" (1 Tim 2:13-14). Here the Pauline author holds a positive view of creation to counteract the Gnostic tendency to consider themselves outside the order of creation. He insists that God's plan for creation, including matter, marriage, sexual intercourse, and procreation must be followed, even after the death and resurrection of Jesus Christ. He cites the order in creation (Gen 2—3) to support his argument that women have an essential role to play. By faithfully carrying it out they attain salvation. Submission to their husbands mirrors the order of creation. Silence in liturigcal assemblies protects the community against Gnostic women teachers.

What happened to the Paul who wrote: "There is neither male nor female; for you are all one in Christ Jesus" (Gal 3:28)? What happened to his vision that men and women were equal, and that their equality was meant to strengthen marriage and childbearing? What happened to the Paul who supported women as leaders in the liturgy and worked side-by-side with women?

After his death, Christians who continued to be drawn to the Gnostic view that they were already risen with Christ claimed to stand outside the order of creation. They understood Paul as denying traditional values in marriage and childbearing, in the beauty of sexual intercourse, and in all distinctions between men and women.

Against these tendencies the mainstream tradition worked to restore "law and order." They adapted the household customs observed in the surrounding culture. They excluded heresy-prone women from liturgical leadership. They stressed the order of creation with wives subordinate to their husbands. Patriarchal patterns from the dominant culture won out over Paul's view of equality with differentiation. Submission, silence, and subordination became watchwords for Christian women, so that the values of sexuality, marriage, and the home might be preserved.

Paul was *not*, therefore, the all-time male chauvinist, nor was he a radical feminist. He was, rather, the one clear voice in the New Testament asserting both the freedom and equality of women and the differences between men and women. Few Christians were able to accept his vision and live within the tension it created. Paul's own tradition soon reinterpreted him according to its own views of creation and the resurrection.

If we are to read Paul afresh, we must separate him from the later Pauline tradition. What is simpler to understand than his vision of equality with differentiation (Gal 3:27-28)? Yet what can be more easily obscured with qualifications? Where might Paul lead us once we listen to his message without prejudice? Hopefully, he might bring us to a freedom in the Spirit for both men and women.